Fitting in is OVERRATED

The Survival Guide for Anyone Who Has Ever Felt Like an Outsider

Leonard Felder, PhD

STERLING

New York / London
www.sterlingpublishing.com

STERLING and the distinctive Sterling logo are registered trademarks of
Sterling Publishing Co., Inc.

Library of Congress Cataloging-in-Publication Data

Felder, Leonard.
  Fitting in is overrated : the survival guide for anyone who has ever felt like an outsider/
Leonard Felder.
     p. cm.
  Includes index.
  ISBN 978-1-4027-4884-4
  1. Individuality. 2. Success--Psychological aspects. I. Title.
  BF697.F445 2008
  158.2--dc22

                              2008013025

10 9 8 7 6 5 4 3 2 1

Published by Sterling Publishing Co., Inc.
387 Park Avenue South, New York, NY 10016
© 2008 by Leonard Felder
Distributed in Canada by Sterling Publishing
C/o Canadian Manda Group, 165 Dufferin Street
Toronto, Ontario, Canada M6K 3H6
Distributed in the United Kingdom by GMC Distribution Services
Castle Place, 166 High Street, Lewes, East Sussex, England BN7 1XU
Distributed in Australia by Capricorn Link (Australia) Pty. Ltd.
P.O. Box 704, Windsor, NSW 2756, Australia

Sterling ISBN 978-1-4027-4884-4

For information about custom editions, special sales, premium and
corporate purchases, please contact Sterling Special Sales
Department at 800-805-5489 or specialsales@sterlingpublishing.com.

To my son, Steven Alon Schorin Felder,
who amazes me each day with his
creativity, courage, and persistence

Acknowledgments

Many people contributed enormously to this book arriving in your hands. Some of these were generous writing teachers and creative partners many years ago: Professors James Michael, Rowland Shepard, and Sean Austin at Kenyon College, as well as Adelaide Bry and Harold Bloomfield in San Diego, who gave me my first writing opportunities.

More recently, I was inspired and guided by several spiritual teachers and beloved friends who offered me honest critiques and caring wisdom, especially Rabbi Miriam Hamrell, Rabbi Ted Falcon, Rabbi Marc Sirinsky, Catherine Coulson, Nancy Pikelny, Lucky Altman, Janet Sternfeld Davis, Teri Bernstein, Peter Reiss, Sandra Kaler, Erica Ruff, Beth Rosenberg, and Harriet Shapiro.

I am fortunate to be part of a loving extended family that includes the Rothenberg Cousins Club in Detroit; my parents, Martin and Ena Felder, in Florida; my siblings, Janice, Andi, Ruthe, and Ron; my brother-in-law, Craig; and my wife's very supportive family, especially Bill Schorin, Jeff Schorin, the Wilstein family, and many cousins across the United States.

Every day I am grateful to live with my very creative and loving wife and best friend, Linda Schorin, and our beloved son, Steven, to whom this book is dedicated.

I also want to thank the women and men who fought for this book and helped it by suggesting important changes and edits. My agent, Stephanie Tade, remained positive, patient, and insightful even when others were getting cold feet. The supportive professionals at Sterling Publishing, including Philip Turner, Dave Nelson, Leigh Ann Ambrosi, Anne Barthel, Hannah Reich, and many others, added their good ideas and strong support for this project.

Most of all, I want to thank the mysterious One, the indefinable Creative Source whose love and guidance has helped me in everything I have written. I hope this book will bring nourishment and support for many other souls who have known the frustration of not fitting in and who also have gifts to offer.

Contents

Chapter One

When Do You Feel Like an Outsider?

Sometimes in the middle of a counseling session, I stop and sit in amazement at the courage, persistence, and creativity of the person sitting in front of me. For many years I've had the privilege of helping a wide variety of remarkable men and women struggle with a dilemma that draws on their deepest resources. It's a dilemma most of us face at some point in our lives—one you may be facing right now. How do you balance the desire to be accepted by the people around you with the desire to follow what's in your heart and soul?

This is the dilemma you face when you're forced to choose between the side of you that wants to play it safe and fit in, and the side of you that is willing to risk being more honest and discovering a more genuine life. It's never an easy choice. If you lean too heavily in the direction of fitting in, your days can become boring, constrained, or depressing. Yet if you lean too far toward being severely honest, you may risk being cut off from certain people and groups you aren't ready yet to live without.

This dilemma is likely to show up in several areas of your life. For example:

✸ *Most people have a deep longing to fit in and be accepted by their families.* But let's be honest about it. Is there someone among your close relatives who is too often opinionated, condescending, or disrespectful toward you or your mate? Is there a parent, sibling, in-law, grown child, or other family member you have tried to please who continues to give you either cold silence or unsolicited advice and criticism? Is there a debate going on in your own mind about whether to say something to this person or keep silent and pretend everything is fine? Possibly you can get through weeks or months without bumping into the painful fact that you are often excluded, criticized, or treated coldly by an important member of your own family. But then a holiday, a wedding, a funeral, a birthday, or an unpleasant phone call puts the issue right back in your face. You find yourself wondering, "Why do I feel so isolated and estranged around some of my own relatives? Will it ever get resolved?"

✸ *Most people have a deep desire to fit in and be accepted in their work lives.* Maybe you fit in pretty well on a day-to-day basis. But then a couple of times each year there's a holiday event or a social gathering where you start to realize you don't feel as connected and included as you'd hoped to be. Maybe a new clique is forming, or the inner circle is shifting, and you're not a part of it. Or possibly a sneaky person is spreading rumors and stirring up tensions as though you're all back in junior high school. Or it might simply be that lately some of your good ideas and suggestions have gotten vetoed by a few narrow-minded insiders who don't like the idea of change. As a result, you're still going through the motions at your job but you don't feel the sense of inclusion or connection you'd like to feel. Is it time to do something to improve your situation, or is it something you feel you must endure without rocking the boat?

✸ *Most people seek a sense of connection with various informal groups of friends and in volunteer activities.* Maybe you've looked for community and friendship at a church or temple, in a nonprofit involvement, or with a particular group of other parents at your child's school. Or maybe you've tried a class, a hobby, an informal gathering in your neighborhood, or a membership in some club or association that you thought might bring a sense of connection. But unfortunately, you sometimes find that the entrenched inner circles in these groups are quite rigid in their way of doing things. You've tried to make suggestions and open things up a bit, but in most cases your ideas get shot down by some inflexible insider who feels threatened because you're invading his or her turf. Who are these rigid folks and how did they become the inner circle? Can you find a way to have greater clout and impact in your personal involvements, or do you simply have to let the stubborn insiders call the shots?

The book you are holding in your hands is *not* about withdrawing into a life of isolation and passivity. Nor is it about spending every waking hour battling with everyone who gets on your nerves. Rather, it's about choosing wisely when to speak your truth and how to say it in a way that gets more positive results than ever. I will show you exactly how an individual like you—creative, thoughtful, unique—can survive and thrive in situations that used to make you shut down or retreat into a shell. I'll give you examples and precise techniques to make sure your good ideas, your outsider perspective, and your creative solutions are respected and taken seriously, even by rigid people who have treated you harshly in the past.

The Problem with Inner Circles

I hope you realize that in most cases it's not your fault if you have been shunned or excluded. One of the unfortunate realities of human life is that certain flawed people (let's not mention any names just yet) become powerful insiders because of who their parents were, whom they went to school with, or how many people they can intimidate.

In addition, many groups—from families to corporations—fall prey to a "group-think" phenomenon that leads them to attack any person or idea that is original, new, or different. Almost like a malfunctioning immune system that tries to kill off anything foreign, they become reflexively defensive or vicious toward anything that isn't blandly familiar and anyone who doesn't fit their narrow mold.

Ironically, many of these groups, families, and organizations suffer, stagnate, or decline because the narrow-minded insiders don't listen to the creative outsiders who simply want to offer valuable insights. The rigid "Status Quo Protectors" are terribly afraid of change, and they often wind up making horrible and self-defeating decisions in their unwillingness to take seriously what the insightful outsiders have to say.

You've probably bumped up against a few of these Status Quo Protectors in your own life. Who comes to mind (in your family, your circle of friends, your workplace, or your outside involvements) as someone who gets defensive whenever you try to offer a good idea for improving things?

This problem is not limited to our extended families, companies, or volunteer groups. It is happening in our society as a whole. I'm hearing from many of my own counseling clients—and from thousands of women and men I've spoken with from all walks of life—that they are distressed to see how our leaders seek only the viewpoints of a narrow group of insiders and their like-minded loyalists. We are living in a time when cautiousness, conformity, and a fear of speaking up are clearly on the rise. Doors of progress that had begun to open are now being closed again. The much-needed voice of the insightful outsider is not being heard.

What Can You Do About It?

I assume you picked up this book because you are a creative individual, a bit of a rebel. You probably don't quite fit the current trend of creeping conformity and narrow thinking. You have experienced personally (or watched a loved one experience) the unfairness of being overruled by someone with an overblown sense of entitlement. You are strong and talented in many areas of your life, but in spite of all your accomplishments there are still moments when you get out-maneuvered by the inner circle.

You probably didn't choose to be an outsider. But what you choose to do right now is the key decision. Will you remain uncomfortable in your own skin, or will you find a realistic way to strengthen your voice and increase your effectiveness in family gatherings, informal groups or important organizations where you've gone unheard in the past? Will you let the stubborn insiders continue to run things their way year after year, or will you find the resources and creativity to make a far greater impact than you ever have?

I can't guarantee how things will turn out, but I can say with complete certainty that I have seen thousands of men and women find a way to stop being excluded and become highly effective in each area of their lives, especially in situations where they were previously cut out of the loop. In each chapter of this book you will discover just how desperately our families, our employers, our informal groups, and our society as a whole need the wisdom and creativity of the insightful outsider. You will learn practical methods to clarify what makes you different and then to transform it into a valuable asset. And you will find that many of our greatest artists, business innovators, creative designers, entrepreneurs, healers, teachers, writers, and courageous leaders are outsiders who learned how to transform their own uniqueness from a liability into a strength.

For just a moment, stop and ask yourself what Ang Lee, Macy Gray, Betty Friedan, Viktor Frankl, Faith Hill, Alex Haley, Antonio Villaraigosa, Elisabeth Kübler-Ross, Charles Schwab, Yo-Yo Ma, and Oprah Winfrey have in common. They are all sensitive individuals who suffered painful exclusion and self-doubt before they found their particular way to thrive as outsiders. They each hit a point in their lives when they had to decide, "Is it more important to fit in, or can I find enough support for expressing the gifts and insights I've discovered as a result of being different from most people?" Their stories and those of many other role models whom I've interviewed for this book—including many of my creative, courageous clients—will give you important clues to making sure your own outsider experiences become the key to your success rather than the reason you're left out.

Do You Have an Outsider's Soul?

A good place to start is to see exactly how much you have in common with other outsiders. Yes, you're still a unique individual. But there are certain shared traits, perspectives, and experiences that can help you discover your gifts and strengths.

To see just how much you have the eyes, ears, heart, and soul of an outsider, please take a moment and decide which of the following sound like you (or someone you care about who is also unlike the majority):

1. Do you have a rare personal quality, a passionate interest, or a creative way of seeing things that certain insiders would judge "different" or "unusual" since it falls outside the narrow range of what they know?
2. Do you sometimes get in hot water because your honesty, your insights, or your outsider's perspective are threatening to certain people who aren't ready to hear the truth?
3. Are you often able to connect with a unique individual whom others don't seem to understand or appreciate?
4. Are you more open than most people to exploring new ideas or trying out solutions that others are afraid are too risky?
5. At work or at family gatherings, do you find that you're reluctant to partake in the pettiness, competitiveness, or mean-spirited comments that others engage in and that this keeps you from fitting in?
6. Do you look around and wonder how certain people know so easily how to be accepted, almost as if they got the instruction book that you never received?
7. Have you ever sensed that your ideas or suggestions are exactly what a particular group needs, but that something about your way of presenting these ideas (or your lack of powerful allies) is causing people to tune you out?
8. As a child, did you ever feel invisible or overlooked in your family or at school because someone else had a dramatic way of grabbing the attention or approval that rarely seemed to come your way?
9. Was there something about your family—perhaps its awkwardness or financial struggles—that caused you to feel "one down" from peers who had more status, clout, or sense of entitlement?
10. Is there something about your appearance, your weight, your way of speaking, or your physical vulnerabilities that sets you apart from others?
11. When spending time with your spouse's or partner's family, or at his or

her work gatherings, have you been treated coldly or felt you simply didn't fit in?

12. Have you sometimes been the "token"—the outnumbered member of your race, gender, religion, sexual orientation, or political leanings—in situations where people said condescending or hurtful things that made it clear you weren't fully accepted?

13. Have you sometimes felt nervous when it's time to sit down for a meal—say, in a school cafeteria or at a dinner party—because you sense it's going to be difficult to find someone to sit with or connect with?

14. In your family of origin, were you the rebel, the one who refused to follow the restrictive life plan that others had set for you?

15. Were you the most honest, sensitive, or aware person in your family of origin, and did you feel that others would rather criticize you than look at their own shortcomings?

If you answered "Yes" to any of the above questions, welcome to the club! By identifying the painful moments you have experienced as an outsider, you are taking a necessary first step toward healing. You are beginning the process of learning more about the traits that previously may have caused you to run away from yourself or shut down emotionally.

Many people are afraid to admit they have been feeling like outsiders, as if it will destroy their chances forever to be successful at work, in social situations, or in family power struggles. They are uncomfortable being unlike the majority, so they start feeling self-conscious in any group situation.

But what if the thing that makes you unlike the majority is actually a strength, a gift, or a source of wisdom that can be turned into an enormous blessing for yourself and others? What if the personal quality you've been insecure about is truly something positive (even if it has been criticized by certain insiders who were too uncomfortable or judgmental to appreciate this aspect of who you are)? What if your greatest breakthrough in life depends on your coming to terms with the very issue that has made you feel shunned?

What to Expect

There are nine chapters remaining in this book. With inspiring true stories and precise steps that you can customize to suit your own particular style, these chapters explore:

⌘ *What held-back gifts, insights, and benefits could you as an outsider now bring forth.* At several points in the pages that follow, I will ask you to dig deeply inside and face the fact that you have probably been holding back some important strength, creative suggestion, or piece of wisdom that might be helpful for others to receive from you. It might be something innovative that can do a lot of good for a particular company, group, nonprofit organization, school, or family situation. But first you will need to find a way to strengthen your voice, develop more support, and make sure you get heard and respected. Even if people aren't open at first to your helpful ideas, we will explore highly productive and positive ways to move them through their resistance so that you can truly be of service.

⌘ *What to say when someone tries to exclude you or cut you out of the loop.* I've found there are clumsy words that can make things worse and there are carefully selected words that can increase the respect you receive and clout you have. In several chapters of this book, you will be given specific tools to stand up for yourself, for your helpful ideas, or for someone else who is being excluded. Instead of being tongue-tied or shut down, you will know how to be much more effective, especially in the most stressful situations.

⌘ *How to avoid the self-sabotage that many outsiders fall into.* Being excluded or shunned can cause you to become excessively self-critical or far too reactive with a chip on your shoulder. In this book, you will learn how to catch yourself *before* you slip into self-criticism or hasty reactions. You will discover specific ways to bring out your most articulate, compassionate, and strong self right at the moments when an insider is getting on your nerves.

⌘ *How to become an excellent mentor, ally, and team member for other outsiders.* Whether it's helping a colleague at work who shares your innovative ideas, or helping a child in your family or your neighborhood who has been teased for being different, you will learn how to become the kind of supportive mentor and guide you may have longed for in your own life. Instead of feeling alone and powerless, you will discover creative ways to gain support for the breakthroughs you seek in your family, your workplace, or in various cliquish groups.

✂ *How to make your circle the one that people want to be in.* In several chapters of this book you will discover realistic ways to attract quality people into your life, either in one-on-one friendships or as newly formed groups of supportive allies. Instead of trying to fit yourself uncomfortably into the narrow mold of an existing clique that has been unwelcoming in the past, you will learn exactly how the most creative and unique individuals are able to carve out better niches of their own in all areas of their lives. Rather than continuing to feel like a fish out of water, you will know precisely how to build strong circles of support, at work or among family and friends, in any stressful situation you face.

A Time-Saving Suggestion

If you have a busy schedule or you're not in the mood to read a book from cover to cover before you can benefit from its ideas, I have some reassuring news: YOU DON'T NEED TO READ ALL TEN CHAPTERS.

To get the most out of this book and to deal more effectively with the stresses in your life, I recommend that you read only the chapters that call out to you from the table of contents. For example, maybe you don't have any outsider issues at work, so you can skip that chapter. Or maybe you no longer feel like an outsider in your own family, so that chapter doesn't really apply to you. If so, feel free to skip it for now and focus on the chapters that do grab your interest.

My goal is not to bog you down, but only to inspire and help you (or someone you know who needs this book). I trust that you will make good decisions about which chapters to omit and which chapters to read and apply to your daily life.

A Personal Note

In addition to being a therapist and advisor for thousands of men and women who learned how to turn their outsider perspectives from deficits into valuable assets, I have been an outsider at several times in my own life. At various points in this book, I will describe what I learned about how to become more resilient and how to make a positive impact even when I felt very different from certain well-positioned or cliquish individuals who were extremely reluctant to hear an outsider's perspective.

My passionate goal for many years in both my professional work and my personal friendships has been to help good people who happen to be different from the pack to reclaim their voice, their strength, and their ability to get things done with integrity. I deeply believe that our families, our workplaces, and our society now more than ever need the wisdom that most outsiders possess. I'm hoping this book will help you make a strong and lasting impact in the areas of your life where you have previously felt blocked or held back.

For years, the Status Quo Preservers and the "insiders by birth" have had their way, and they've made a mess of things. It's time for the insightful outsiders to make the next move and start to repair the damage. Whether it's at your next family get-together, your next department meeting at work, or the next planning session of your church, temple, or volunteer group, someone with vision and guts needs to be heard. Are you interested in making that happen? If so, let's explore together how to do it well.

Chapter Two

Why It's So Uncomfortable to Stand Apart

Before we go deeply into practical solutions for dealing with cliques and closed doors, we first need to check in with your gut and your heart. For just a brief moment, let's explore what it feels like to be outnumbered or cut out of the loop at work, in groups, or with your family.

Picture this: It's a hectic morning at work and an important decision is being made that will affect your future. But you weren't invited to a key meeting and a group of insiders makes the decision without your input.

Then at the end of the day it's finally time to sit down with loved ones and break bread. Where is the close, connected group around you? Maybe you live alone or with a cat whose attitude is, "Hey, I come from Egyptian royalty and you think I'm supposed to give you the time of day?"

Or maybe you live with several humans, but one of them is working late again. Or one member of your family is on the phone or the computer and doesn't want to join you for dinner. Or someone is physically at the table but somewhere else emotionally. You long to connect, but the connection isn't happening.

After dinner, you go to a meeting, a class, or the gathering of a group you have participated in for quite a while. As you walk in, you notice that the cliquish insiders are already glomming onto each other and shutting you out. You offer several good ideas at the meeting, but your ideas get shot down by a few people who listen only to their like-minded favorites. You had hoped to find a sense of belonging in this group, but in fact it seems to stir up old feelings of being left out and alone.

Admitting the Truth

At these uncomfortable moments when you sense you are being judged, left out, or treated coldly, your brain may be insisting, "Ignore them. They're not that important. You don't need their approval."

But let's be honest. If you check in with your gut and your heart, is there something that feels unsettled or unfair? Do you carry a lingering worry deep inside that maybe you just don't know the way to be accepted and appreciated in these unbending groups of people?

If you get treated as though you don't matter or your good ideas don't count, it *does* hurt! You'd be lying to yourself or visiting that overcrowded State of Denial if you said to yourself, "Hey, I'm fine. Just pass me the box of cookies."

In this chapter, we will uncover what really happens inside your emotions when you get cast aside by people you thought were your friends, allies, or trusted relatives. As you read the descriptions on the next several pages, examine them honestly to see which ones you have experienced personally and which ones apply to someone you care about who has also known the sting of being treated like an outsider.

Issue #1: You'll probably feel tempted to stoop to the level of the people who are mistreating you

I'll admit it's not easy keeping your composure when you are faced with insensitive remarks or harsh criticism. When someone at work, in a social group, or in your family talks about you in a hurtful way or acts as if you don't count, you may feel a quick flash of anger or an urge to get back at this person. While your feelings of anger are probably justified, you still need to choose wisely on how to respond. As I'm sure you'll agree, an impulsive choice that makes things worse is not such a great idea.

But let's be honest about what goes on in stressful moments. Every day, well-educated, reasonable, and thoughtful individuals nevertheless have moments when they feel pushed to the edge emotionally. When someone at work, in a clique, or in your family treats you like you are irrelevant or invisible, you might be tempted to just "go off" because your anger has been building up for far too long. Especially on a project or a goal for which you are passionately involved, when someone deliberately cuts you out of the loop or slams your good ideas in public, do you feel the heat rise inside your stomach, your chest, and your face?

Does that ever happen to you? Even—or especially—if you are basically a patient, kind, and sensible person, is there one snobby group or one hurtful individual whose rudeness gets under your skin over and over again? Do you sometimes find yourself building up so much resentment that you're on the verge of lashing out or making a scene?

You may be saying to yourself, "No way. I would never stoop to yelling or going off on someone at work or at a family gathering, even if they were being rude or dismissive." Fine, I'll take your word for it, you're not a yeller. But you might notice that at certain stressful moments you speak in a highly *controlled* tone of voice, so filled with bitterness and self-righteousness that it comes across as even more insulting than screaming or yelling. You might think you're above it all because you use "rational" arguments and fancy words, but the anger and frustration are leaking out nonetheless and dripping all over your crisply pressed clothes.

Even though your frustration is probably justified, the patronizing and lecturing almost always make things worse, especially if you plan on staying in the same job, family, or group where this frustrating person will remain a part of your life. Once you've spilled your feelings of contempt—rightly or wrongly—on this person, it's hard to see each other in the office or show up at the same family gatherings year after year.

Or maybe, instead of stooping to the level of your tormentors, you choose another unfortunate option: you stay silent and passive, and in the process give yourself lower back pain and a jaw so tight with resentment that you'll end up needing surgery for TMJ syndrome. (The temporo-mandibular joint pain that afflicts many people who insist "I'm fine, I'll just grit my teeth and ignore it.") I've found in thousands of cases that the person who "sucks it up" is actually churning out stomach acid, fraying nerve endings, and clenching muscles on a daily basis. The person who remains silent and composed during daylight hours is often up late at night with racing thoughts or cravings for food.

Since neither extreme—the anger-unloading or the anger-suppressing—works very well in most cases, what are your other, better options? What will help you regain your inner strength and your clarity of mind when you are feeling outnumbered, left out, or mistreated?

A POWERFUL MANTRA

I've found that in order to respond effectively to someone who is treating you rudely, the first essential step is to stop for a moment and make a promise to yourself: "I'm going to handle this with decency and integrity no matter what." Thousands of clients have found that just this one silently spoken sentence can give great strength and clarity during a stressful moment. This powerful vow or mantra can snap you out of the victim mentality and into a sense of creativity and strength. Rather than stooping to the other person's level, your mind begins to feel clearer, better able to handle a tough situation with dignity and grace.

For example, my client Eileen is one of the kindest and most compassionate individuals you will ever meet, but she can get snippy and short-tempered if she feels pushed too far by people who treat her in a hurtful way. Eileen has a tremendous capacity for sensing what other people are feeling or needing. This gift of empathy has helped her enormously in her work as the program director of a social services agency. Her compassion, however, tends to run out when she's repeatedly ignored, left out, or treated rudely.

When she first came to me for counseling, Eileen admitted, "I'm usually so focused on what other people want and how to keep everyone from getting upset. But then when someone repeatedly takes advantage of my niceness, or when I give too much and I start to burn out, I sometimes get to the point where I'm real close to the edge." Eileen sought therapy because she *was* starting to burn out. She was bending over backward for her somewhat self-absorbed husband and her extremely volatile teenage daughter. She said, "I used to feel close to and very trusting of my husband and my daughter. But lately they are both so focused on their own needs and their endless personal dramas, I feel like I'm a bystander in my own family."

She was also beginning to feel concerned about the new executive director at the nonprofit agency where she had worked for many years. According to Eileen, this woman was a rigid perfectionist with an irritating habit of leaving Eileen out of major decisions and refusing to listen to her insights about important daily problems with staff and clients. As Eileen explains, "For many years I loved this job, but lately I feel as if the new executive director is running a one-woman show and the rest of us are just supposed to carry her props and do her bidding."

Like many compassionate people I've counseled over the years, Eileen was intelligent and well-informed on many topics, but she admitted she was clueless as to how to deal with the insensitive, self-absorbed, and stubborn individuals in her life who played by a different set of rules. Each night she was having trouble sleeping because of the discomfort in her back, the tightness in her shoulders, or her frequent digestive upsets. She also had been told by two specialists that she might need surgery to correct the tightness in her jaw.

But even more damaging to Eileen's heart and soul was the fact that she was beginning to question her own right to her concerns. As she told me during her initial counseling session, "I'm starting to think I'm just too weak or too sensitive to deal with inflexible people like my teenager daughter, my self-centered husband, and my perfectionist boss. I wish I could just suck it up and get over it like I see other people do. I wish I didn't have so much turmoil inside me—that I could just go zombie-like through the motions of living without so much pain and discomfort."

Like many remarkable and gifted individuals who feel burned-out from living in an increasingly harsh world, Eileen was almost ready to trade in her own compassionate nature if it might mean having less pain and frustration on a daily basis. During her second counseling session, she asked me (half in jest), "Isn't there some magic pill that could help me be less sensitive?"

I told Eileen about one of my favorite teachers, the famous neurologist and psychiatrist Dr. Viktor Frankl, and what I'd learned from him about how to deal effectively with hurtful and insensitive individuals. I had read his books in college, then studied with him in person a few years later. A brilliant, compassionate, and always curious individual, Frankl was a young man in Vienna, married with a growing career, when he and his relatives were captured by the Nazis and taken to concentration camps. He lost his wife, brother, mother, and father in the camps. He was sent eventually to Auschwitz, where food rations were extremely scarce and each day was brutal.

Based on his personal experience of surviving the worst treatment imaginable, which he described in *Man's Search for Meaning* and *The Doctor and the Soul*, Frankl taught that the best way to stay sane when you are surrounded by insensitive or uncaring individuals—as well as to protect your own heart and soul—is to search each day to find moments of decency and integrity even when certain others around you are giving up on their own sense of humanity. In the concentration camps, Frankl made sure to find a sense of purpose, a sense of kindness, a sense of humor, and a sense of inner mindfulness that gave him strength and endurance. No matter how ugly the behavior of the guards and prisoners around him, he looked for ways to be of service to at least one other human being every day. His passionate search for creative solutions to his situation began with listening to the wisdom of his own gut, heart, and soul.

I said to Eileen, as I've said to many other at-risk men and women struggling to keep up their strength when surrounded by hurtful or self-absorbed individuals, "Make sure that each day you take a moment to honor your own truth, your own inner wisdom, and the longings of your soul. Even if you can't control some of the ways your teenage daughter, your husband, and your boss behave, you *can* control the fact that you are living each day with your creativity and your humanity intact."

Eileen began to accomplish this by saying to herself at crucial moments, "I'm going to handle this situation with decency and integrity no matter what." She also began to write in a private journal each day, for a few minutes in the morning and a few minutes in the evening, to stay strong and focused despite whatever challenges her husband, her daughter, or her boss were giving her. I've seen powerful results when clients like Eileen set aside just a few minutes of private journal writing time each day to come up with creative strategies to handle even the most irritating situations with decency and integrity. For those who don't feel comfortable writing in a private journal, I have asked them instead to set aside a few moments at least once a day for prayer, meditation, taking a brief walk in nature, talking with a supportive friend, or having a conversation with their own hearts. Each human being has a different and unique way to reconnect with his or her strength—the key is finding and honoring your own particular method.

For example, you may find—whether or not you're religious—that creative prayers and meditations can assist you in keeping your integrity strong and your creativity alive even when you have to deal with extremely hurtful individuals. Here is one prayer that I've found works exceptionally well regardless of your beliefs or background: take a deep breath in and out as you say, "Please open my heart and give me strength to make sure I respond with firmness and decency here. Show me a way to be effective, strong, and kind at the same time."

In later chapters we will explore many more ways to respond well to cliquish, hurtful, and insensitive people. I'll go into detail about what works (and what doesn't work) when standing up for yourself with a boss, colleague, friend, lover, relative, or stranger who treats you rudely or shuts you out. But for now, let's focus on the first steps for checking in with your gut, your heart, and your soul to make sure you don't stoop to the level of those around you.

In Eileen's case, these first steps included writing in her journal, saying a quick re-centering prayer, and reminding herself right at the most upsetting moments, "I'm going to handle this situation with decency and integrity no matter what." These three additions to her daily routine made a huge difference in how she responded effectively to her husband, her daughter, and her boss when things got stressful.

I've found that the success of your response to a rude or dismissive person depends almost entirely on whether you can connect with your own center and gain access to your own inner strength right at the moment when this person is challenging you. In your own difficult moments, how will you deal best with the feelings of discomfort that are stirring inside you—the irritations and concerns that you can no longer ignore? Rather than trying to stuff your feelings inside, where they'll accumulate and eventually explode, what might be a safe and appropriate way to honor your own inner wisdom? Would you prefer to use a private journal (that you make sure no one you live with or work with is going to read)? Or would you prefer to spend a few minutes in prayer, meditation, check-in phone calls with a friend, or silent conversations with your own heart?

Issue #2: It Hurts to Get Left Out Because Human Beings Are Hard-Wired to Seek a Sense of Belonging Somewhere

Even if you consider yourself a loner, a rebel, or someone who can survive quite well on your own, there is still a part of you—as there is of each of us—that longs for connection. When you go for weeks, months, or years without sufficient human warmth, or emotional support, it can damage your physical health and your emotional well-being.

Research shows that the need for connection and for a place to belong is a basic trait in most mammals and especially in humans. A few of the scientific studies are listed in the Sources, Notes, and Recommended Readings in the back of this book.

But just to give you some food for thought, let's consider the common thread that is found in some of the highest-rated television series of the past few decades. It's no accident that the scenarios that draw the largest audiences are those that create a sense of belonging and connection for people who feel different or excluded. For example, the extremely popular *Cheers* was about a dependable gathering of unusual characters who found a place "where everybody knows your name." *Friends, Seinfeld, Will and Grace, Sex and the City*, and *Grey's Anatomy* are also about unconventional people who don't fit in easily within a conventional world, but find a replacement family where they can check in frequently and sort out what's going on in their daily lives.

Yet as much as we all long to feel connected, welcomed, and included somewhere, there are still going to be situations where we get treated like persona non grata, a Latin phrase that literally means "unwelcome or unacceptable person." If you stop and seriously think about this phrase for a moment, you will realize that being "unacceptable or unwelcome" depends entirely on the viewpoint of the person who is excluding you. Some judgmental, snobby, or intolerant person has decided who belongs and who doesn't, who gets treated well and who might as well be invisible.

Now here's an interesting biological fact: In most mammalian species, as it was in most ancient human tribes, to be shunned by the tribal insiders and to be cut out of the loop on food supply and protection is tantamount to death. As a result, we humans are hard-wired with a physiological response that kicks in when we feel left out or excluded. We experience a primal sense of shame or danger. While the logical frontal cortex may realize that the clique's behavior is absurd and should be of no consequence to us, our survival-oriented lower brain quickly fires off a burst of adrenalin, a head-to-toe warning signal that says, "Oh, no! I'd better not get left out. I won't survive if I'm cut off from the food (money, success, love, attention, approval) I can't live without."

That's why during a moment of getting teased, shunned, or disregarded, your face quickly turns red, your heart races, and your entire body feels a little strange, as if you have been "found out" or "dangerously left behind." The adrenalin is pumping and the dread can be quite intense for even the most well-adjusted and rational individuals. This feeling of danger (especially if it happens repeatedly) can stick in your memory and have a serious impact on your physical and mental health.

Here's an illustration of how this works in modern life: A very intelligent and hard-working client of mine, named Artie, comes from a family where he was often criticized and put down by his competitive, sarcastic older siblings. Both of Artie's parents are also quite verbally aggressive. His mom is a high-powered lawyer and his dad is an agent in Hollywood.

In Artie's family, it's always been considered perfectly normal to pick at one another and poke fun at anything that makes a family member appear vulnerable or sensitive. Artie's two brothers and his sister developed a very tough exterior to deal with this kind of upbringing. But for Artie, who's a gentle soul and a much less competitive individual at heart, it was a painful family to grow up in, and he still finds it hard to connect with his sarcastic and cynical siblings, who have all succeeded in high-powered and lucrative careers.

For many years, Artie struggled with depression and self-critical thoughts partly as a result of being so much less affluent and successful than his driven siblings and parents. At one point during his early thirties, when he was laid off from a job he had hoped would last a long time, Artie even thought about suicide. Fortunately, a close friend talked him into seeking help, and he's made enormous progress in the past several years. Yet despite all the things that are going well in his life now, his parents and his siblings still view him as a "disappointment."

What no one in this particular family has been willing (or able) to recognize is that by almost any measure, Artie is an outstanding human being. If you were to spend time with Artie and his relatives, you would know for certain that Artie is the one family member who knows how to listen and truly cares about people. While others in the family have much more impressive resumes, investment portfolios, and social calendars, Artie is the one you'd call in a crisis to come over and help you out with solid advice and genuine friendship. He's the one person in the family who has a healthy long-term relationship and treats his partner as a true equal. Artie currently works as an occupational therapist who does an amazing job helping stroke patients and kids with autism and sensory disorders. But in the eyes of his status-conscious relatives, he is still a "loser."

Now let me ask you what I asked Artie about his persona non grata role in his family. Is there something truly wrong with Artie that he has devoted his life to helping others? Or is there something wrong with his family members' belief that Artie is a "loser" and a "disappointment" because he has a different set of values than they do?

Certainly, it's a free country and you can vote for any perspective that feels true for you. You might feel in your gut that anyone who chooses to help elderly people recovering from strokes, or kids with autism and sensory disorders, is not a classy enough addition to your next elegant dinner party. On the other hand, you might feel deeply that you'd rather spend an evening talking to Artie than to his highly influential but extremely cynical and sarcastic family members. You get to decide. Your decision will reveal whether you are open to the ways of the outsider or whether it irritates you that someone could be so naïve as to put human contact and personal service ahead of affluence and status.

Now let me ask you one more question. Regardless of whether you think Artie is an outstanding person or a loser, I would like you to think about how you view your own worth as a human being. Have you taken to heart the criticism and demeaning comments of certain people in your life who never appreciated your way of being because it differed from what they valued? Have you been paying a high physical or emotional price for the narrow or rigid beliefs of someone in your family, your workplace, or your social group who has never liked you or what you stand for? Do you recover quickly from flashes of fear or self-consciousness when you find yourself judged or excluded? Or have you lost sight of your own gifts and your own essential goodness because others have insisted repeatedly that you are not living up to their standards?

I've always loved this line from Eleanor Roosevelt: "No one can make you feel inferior without your consent." Being different from the pack will continue to be painful if you are consenting to those others' narrow views of what matters in life. But you can begin to heal and regain your strength if you realize that your gifts, as well as your unconventional way of being, are just as needed in this broken world as those of any "insider."

Issue #3: It Hurts to Be Shunned Because You Are Unsure of Whether to Stand Up for Someone Else Who's on the Outside

There is one more facet of discomfort that we need to discuss. It's the moment when you find yourself in an awkward or vulnerable spot because someone you care about is being excluded or demeaned. Here are a few illustrations from my counseling practice and personal life.

Jeanette is a rising star where she works because she is extremely talented and dedicated to her job. But she's in a bind because her closest friend at work, a creative and edgy rebel named Karen, is somewhat of an outcast in the office.

According to Jeanette, "I find Karen a terrific person to know, with a great sense of humor, and she's very talented at what she does. But since Karen is not very politically savvy at work, she is viewed as a bit of a loose cannon by my boss and several of the most powerful and influential people we work with. I often feel unsure about whether to stand up for Karen or protect my own standing here."

Jeanette admits, "There's a part of me that knows I ought to defend Karen because even when she's a bit clumsy in her choice of words or her timing, she is still spot-on-accurate most of the time and she sees things that others haven't seen yet. Yet there's another part of me that knows I can't afford to make too many waves here, or lean too far in the direction of sticking up for Karen, because I'll be perceived as less loyal to the boss's inner circle that has so much clout here where we work."

Bruce comes from a family where there are strict rules about what's acceptable and what's not, especially when it comes to religious issues. A few years ago, Bruce's younger brother Kevin announced to the family that he was going to convert to a different religion. Bruce's parents and grandparents were deeply hurt by this and angry at Bruce for supporting his brother.

As Bruce explains, "I love my parents and I respect the fact that their religious beliefs are central to who they are. But at the same time, I feel trapped in a no-win situation because I'm also very close to Kevin and I can understand why he feels strongly about his decision to pursue the spiritual path that means so much to him. Sometimes during phone calls and family visits I feel like the wishbone at Thanksgiving dinner being pulled apart."

Catherine is the mother of a young girl named Elana, a very creative and sensitive child. Elana has some delays in reading and some social awkwardness, and she's often excluded from play-dates and group activities at her school. This has caused a lot of discomfort for Catherine.

"Not only is it painful to see my daughter's frustrations at not fitting in at school and in after-school activities," she says, "but I often get these strange looks from other moms who treat me as a bit of a pariah because of my daughter's difficulties. Sometimes when I'm picking up my daughter at school and I get the silent treatment or the insincere hellos from other moms, I feel like saying, 'Would you all just grow up and stop this who's in and who's out game that is so last century? Can we all just help each other out and get rid of the competitive nonsense?'"

During her first counseling session, however, Catherine began to explore why she freezes up and says nothing around these other moms. "Most of the time I get tongue-tied and I don't know exactly how to stand up for myself or my daughter. A feeling of shame runs through me and it's as though I'm back in junior high school."

I asked Catherine, "What was it like when you were in junior high?"

She paused for a moment and then told me what I have often heard from men and women who look back with dread at the exclusion they experienced in their teenage years. "When I was in eighth grade, I looked horrible," Catherine said. "I was going through all sorts of physical changes with hormones and weight problems. My skin was a mess. I was starting to get crushes on boys, but I was four inches taller than most of the boys and my chest was flatter than a board.

"In my school, there was this one group of girls that seemed to have a lock on who was acceptable and who was going to be teased. I had been close friends with one of the three girls in that clique—we lived on the same block from the time we were in first grade—but in eighth grade she got cold and vicious. One day I was in school and starting to give a presentation in my social studies class. I began to hear whispering and giggles at the back of the room where the three powerful girls always sat. Within a few minutes, the entire class was laughing at me and I didn't know why. Then I looked down and saw a tiny piece of bathroom tissue stuck to my shoes."

Sitting in my office, Catherine shook her head in amazement. "It's been many years since that incident, but when I see Elana getting left out or I feel excluded by the other moms, it's as though I'm right back in eighth grade with something stuck on my shoes and the cliquish girls laughing at me."

It took several months in therapy for Catherine to fully sort out how this incident and several other painful moments from her past were holding her back from being the strong and articulate advocate that she wanted to be for her daughter. But to her credit, Catherine did the inner work and came up with some brilliant ways to get the support services and remedial help her daughter needed. (For more information, see the Recommended Readings at the end of this book.) She also made enormous progress in discovering how to deal with rude moms at school and how to find allies and teammates for raising kids with special needs.

If there is something from your own past that is causing you to be especially vulnerable to the rudeness, coldness, or insensitivity of others, I'm hoping that this book will help you resolve these painful memories. All of us have some incidents in our past that can trigger us to freeze up and get tongue-tied when we are treated like unwelcome outsiders. Yet all of us have the potential to work through these barriers (either on our own or with a supportive counselor or therapist) and to become stronger in standing up for ourselves and our loved ones whenever someone acts in a cruel or dismissive way.

I urge you to read on in order to discover some inspiring examples and easy-to-follow strategies for responding better when you feel like an outsider. It will help your gut and your heart to heal from the painful moments of exclusion you have experienced. And it will give you the strength and clarity to succeed in any situation where you stand apart.

Chapter Three

The Benefits of Being Positively Different

Here comes some good news. In the next several pages, I will describe four specific gifts and benefits that are available to you as a result of your having an outsider's perspective.

I urge you to read this "Benefits Package" carefully to see which of these apply to you and which might apply to someone you live with, work with, or mentor. I have seen thousands of examples of diverse men and women bringing each of the following possibilities to fruition. I'm hoping they will happen in your life as well.

Benefit #1: After Experiencing the Pain of Being an Outsider, You Might Come Up with Creative Solutions that the Insiders Don't See

Someone who's had the experience of being left out may gain the perspective and persistence it takes to bring about important change. Just as the inside of an oyster shell requires a tremendous amount of friction and irri-tation in order to form an exquisite pearl, there is something about the pain of the outsider that contains the possibility of major insights and creative breakthroughs.

Let me give you an example that will illustrate how the pain of being ostracized can become the necessary friction that creates an amazing benefit for both the insightful outsiders and the stubborn insiders. It's a story that may surprise you—a true story about an unforgettable woman I met in Los Angeles many years ago who told me in great detail about an important turning point in her thinking and her life's work.

THE WOMAN WHO WASN'T SMILEY ENOUGH FOR THE SORORITIES

Long before she became famous, the woman's name was Bettye Goldstein. At the workshop and discussion where I first met her, she explained how, at Central High School in Peoria, Illinois, the make-or-break test of whether you were popular—"good enough"—came during fraternity and sorority pledge week in sophomore year. Bettye desperately wanted to be accepted into the most prestigious girls' sorority, which had not only the best social events but also the most clout on campus.

Bettye had been warned by both of her parents and several of her class-mates that the best way to gain acceptance would be to hold back somewhat on her own intelligence and intensity. Even though Bettye was an extremely smart, curious, creative, and thoughtful person, her mom had lectured her repeatedly, "You've got to stop bringing home so many books from the library and you've got to stop raising your hand so often in class and expressing your opinions. It alienates the other girls and it intimidates the boys. No man is going to want to marry a girl who keeps showing she is smarter than he is."

In truth, Bettye's mom was also intelligent and opinionated, but like most women of her generation she had learned to keep herself in check and to avoid bringing up serious topics outside of the home. In order to be acceptable in Peoria as the respectable wife of a hard-working man who devoted long hours to running a jewelry store, Bettye's mom had focused on keeping an immaculately clean house, picking out the right furnishings, wearing the best fashions, joining the right social clubs, and perfecting the art of makeup and jewelry.

On the surface, Bettye's mom had pulled it off—she was accepted by many of the most powerful insiders in Peoria. Yet she and Bettye's father were terrified that their too-serious, too-smart daughter would never have any friends or any chance at marriage if she didn't stop being so obviously bookish and independent and start being a lot more fashion-conscious and deferential.

The day of the sorority selection arrived. Bettye held her breath waiting for the phone to ring. But it never rang. No explanation was given, yet the message was clear.

When Bettye spoke many years later about the discomfort of trying to fit in during high school, I could see in her expressive eyes that the pain of being excluded was still a vivid memory for her. She admitted that she used to stare out the window of her room at night, especially on Friday and Saturday evenings when she was home alone, crying herself to sleep with thoughts of the parties, sleepovers, and friendships she was missing because she had been rejected by the popular groups at Central High.

"I knew quite clearly that in order to be accepted and liked," Bettye explained, "you had to be thin, smiley, polite, perfectly dressed, and never outspoken about anything substantial, especially about wanting to change the way things were." Bettye also knew she was never going to be thin enough, cheery enough, or superficial enough. As early as age fourteen, she had begun to feel self-conscious about the fact that despite her parents' warnings, she was still bookish, opinionated, Jewish, creative, and passionate about repairing what was unjust in the world.

For many years afterward, Bettye Goldstein struggled with this painful self-consciousness. For a while she tried to do what her mother had done—to hold back some of her intelligence and intensity in order to find happiness living through the achievements of her husband. But eventually she also tried on her own to break into the male-dominated worlds of academics, journalism, and social research. You probably know her by her married name: Betty Friedan.

Like many outsiders I have spoken with over the past few decades, Betty spent most of her teenage and young adult years thinking that she was the only one who was feeling the severe pain of not fitting in. This is a trick the mind plays on us when we feel shunned or isolated. The anxious brain almost always assumes we are the only individual it's happening to. It rarely, if ever, takes into account the crucial fact that the cliquish insiders have excluded not just us but somewhere between 70 percent and 99 percent of the interesting, fascinating, and valuable men and women who didn't fit the insiders' rigid notion of who belongs in the inner circle. The rejected person's brain and heart silently insist, "There must be something wrong with me and this rejection proves it."

Has your anxious, self-critical brain ever played that trick on you? Have you ever walked into a meeting or a social event and felt self-conscious because you assumed you were the only outsider, then later learned there were many individuals who were just as new to or different from the group as you were? Have you ever felt hurt because you assumed you were the only person being left out of a selection process or an important activity, then learned there were all sorts of original thinkers and rebellious characters being excluded? Have you ever judged yourself and said, "This rejection proves I don't have what it takes," then learned the rejection had more to do with other factors and nothing to do with your true worth?

What I find most interesting about Betty Friedan's life story is that she could have done what millions of other women of her generation did. She could have shut down emotionally and retreated into a life of cautious conformity. She could have thrown up her hands in discouragement and said, "What's the point of trying to change something that is never going to change?"

But instead she made up her mind that she was going to dig deeper and learn why her classmates were so afraid of having strong opinions about important issues or showing their intelligence in public. She was also going to find out why her parents kept fighting so often about money and control. Beginning in her final years of high school in Peoria and continuing through her college days at Smith in Northampton, Massachusetts, Betty began doing research into how women secretly felt about their lives and their options.

She used her training as a journalist to interview as many women as she could find who would talk to her. She began writing articles for her college newspaper, and eventually for various magazines, about the things that women felt in their hearts but were afraid to admit out loud. Rather than feeling isolated or embarrassed for having a good mind and a strong sense of rebellious curiosity, Betty began to reach out and seek allies who also wanted to explore the suppressed insights and the hushed voices of women who had been told to dress pretty and be seen but not heard.

These studies of women at various ages and stations in life eventually led to an outspoken book that most publishing experts thought would do poorly in the marketplace because it was more like a research project or a scholarly essay than a mass-market page-turner. The hardcover sales were meager. But to the surprise of many, *The Feminine Mystique* took off in paperback and eventually reached millions of women and men with a startling new idea: that there were many women who wanted more out of life than living through their husbands, and that these women wanted to use their smarts in ways that had long been out of reach.

So the rejected and isolated Bettye Goldstein from Peoria became one of the most famous and influential figures of the second half of the twentieth century. Instead of staying a silenced outsider, she learned to speak with conviction and passion in front of thousands. She helped found the National Organization for Women, the National Women's Political Caucus, and several other organizations that were devoted to opening up doors for women.

As a result of Betty's passionate efforts and those of her many colleagues, there is a long list of professions that were essentially closed to women before 1965 but that gradually began to include women at their highest levels of leadership: medicine, law, scientific research, business management, finance, engineering, space travel, academia, and government, to name just a few. Betty's work to encourage women to start their own businesses not only inspired millions of women in North America, but also helped millions of other women and families worldwide to break out of centuries of poverty, dependence, and abuse. In addition, Betty's persistent efforts to get people thinking about marriage as a partnership between equals—though terrifying to some—was helpful to millions of men and women who benefited from the changes that began to take place in families in many parts of the world.

Certainly she was not perfect. Many women and men who knew Betty much better than I did have told me she could be impatient, intolerant, and impulsive at times. Yet she came a very long way—from the young girl crying herself to sleep at night, feeling all alone, to the courageous spark and creative strategist on the front lines of major societal change. Quite often in my own life, when I am facing a tough decision about whether to speak up regarding something that is unfair or unjust, I think back to the moments when I looked into the serious and sad eyes of Betty Friedan. I think to myself, "There's no way Betty would let this one slide. It's time to take a deep breath and do something positive to change what clearly needs to be changed."

More than anything else, Betty Friedan's story is about making sure your voice and your ideas get heard, regardless of whether you have an XY or an XX pair of chromosomes. In your own life, is there some situation at work, in a group, or with your family that needs a bit of her courage and creativity to keep you or others from getting treated in an unfair manner? Is there some way to turn the discomfort of being excluded into a source of strength and persistence for making important changes that you can envision more vividly than almost anyone else? As Betty Friedan's example proves, you don't have to be perfect; you might even get called the "B word" and some other nasty names. But are you willing to do your part in repairing some aspect of your corner of the world that you know in your heart needs fixing?

Benefit #2: An Outsider Perspective Can Be an Important Advantage in Your Business or Career

If you have a creative imagination or an original way of solving problems, someone is going to reject you for it. But someone else is going to benefit from the fact that your expansive mind can think in an unconventional way and resolve issues that more linear thinkers can't figure out.

Having an original or unconventional mind might have caused you trouble during your school years or in your first few jobs when bosses wanted you to be compliant and not to rock the boat too much. But at some point in your life, the outsider perspective that got you branded as rebellious may become the key to your greatest successes.

For example, did you know that Charles Schwab struggled throughout grade school, college, and graduate school with severe dyslexia? Like most men and women with this reading disorder, he felt embarrassed at not being able to read fluently and he tried to hide from his friends and teachers the fact that he was having a very difficult time with homework and class assignments.

Yet Charles Schwab's dyslexic brain, which doesn't think in straight lines but rather jumps to places that a linear brain wouldn't be able to go, turned out to be the key to his enormous success in the world of finance. He constantly comes up with new and innovative ways to improve customer service, to break the stuffy rituals of investing, and to increase the overall effectiveness of his discount brokerage firm, Charles Schwab and Company, which was an unwelcome outsider on Wall Street until it began to outperform and dramatically surpass most of the long-standing investment houses.

Paul Orfalea, the founder of Kinko's, had a terrible time getting through school because his brain was so imaginative, nonlinear, and creative; now he's a multimillionaire after selling Kinko's to FedEx. John Chambers, the CEO of computer giant Cisco Systems, traces his passion for making information processing user-friendly to the various learning disabilities he struggled with as a child. Mrs. Fields of cookie fame, who was brilliant at marketing, publicity, recipes, and customer service, struggled painfully with math and number-crunching. There are thousands of highly successful business leaders who felt left behind or set apart in school because their brains had different strengths than those the standardized tests were addressing.

Just because someone thinks differently from the majority, it doesn't mean he or she isn't brilliant or valuable. In fact, some of the most important corporate decisions require the fresh eyes and the unique ideas of an original thinker. If you or someone you care about has a brain that can't do certain routine tasks, but can think boldly and unconventionally to solve workplace dilemmas and creative issues, your challenge is to find the right organization and the right supportive teammates that can help these unique gifts to flourish.

THE WOMAN WHO COULDN'T SIT STILL

One of my favorite examples of a person who discovered how being different could be turned to advantage is the explorer, scientist, and teacher Ann Bancroft (no relation to the actress Anne Bancroft from *The Graduate*, whose real name was Anna Maria Louisa Italiano). This Ann Bancroft grew up in Minnesota and felt isolated from her classmates for several reasons. First, she was extremely energetic and athletic, but there was no Title IX funding yet for girls' athletics and there were no organized programs except cheerleading to help young women do something positive with all their energy. A young woman was supposed to "sit still" and "be a lady," but Ann Bancroft had far more life force inside her than the average kid, so she was labeled hyperactive and considered a "problem."

The second reason for Ann's sense of isolation was the fact that she had a learning disability. In seventh grade, when young teens are most concerned about fitting in and being part of the group, she was put in a special-education class. She recalls feeling ashamed and frustrated that her learning difficulties made the other kids tease her and judge her harshly.

The third reason for Ann's sense of isolation was that her schoolgirl crushes were on *women*. This was before there was much mainstream awareness of, or support for, living openly and letting others know who you really are. So Ann learned to build a rich inner world for herself, living in her imagination and keeping quiet about what was most important to her.

This could have been the start of a depressing life, but that's not what happened. Like many outsiders who simply refuse to accept that being different is a deficit, Ann Bancroft turned her reasons for being isolated into tremendous advantages for the adult portion of her time on earth. First, she worked hard to become more proficient at reading, eventually becoming a teacher in Minnesota. Second, she pursued her dream of being an explorer and used her energy and wanderlust to become the first woman to cross the continent of Antarctica on foot. In the ninety-four days it took to cross 1,700 miles of icy expanse (with treacherous crevasses all around) by walking or using skis and ski sails, Ann and her fellow explorer, Liv Arnesen from Norway, accomplished several amazing things. Not only did they survive in icy climates where exposed skin would freeze in less than a minute, they also managed to work as reliable teammates and save each other's lives on several occasions, despite their substantial cultural differences, contrasting communication styles, and different sexual orientations.

Ann Bancroft accomplished this by putting together a team of corporate sponsors, communication experts, and scientific education specialists who helped her set up a live connection with more than three million children from sixty-five countries who tuned in via satellite phones and logged on to Ann's Web site to follow her progress, ask questions, and make suggestions. All across the globe, thousands of Girl Scout troops, science classes, computer labs, and homerooms of every race and ethnicity tuned in daily to learn from Ann's originality, courage, and practicality.

While Ann began her life feeling embarrassed about being sent to special ed, she became in effect one of the most influential and well-known educators on the planet. Right now there are millions of children, teens, and young adults who have developed a passion for science, exploration, communication technology, and team building because they were part of this first-of-its-kind interactive Web community that Ann devised in her innovative mind.

I hope these stories of men and women who turned their sense of exclusion into creative and innovative career strengths will inspire you or someone you know. In my counseling practice, I often meet people who aren't sure how to bounce back from the criticism, rejection, or isolation they have experienced as a result of being different. I can't guarantee how things will turn out for you, but I have found repeatedly that inside nearly every person who doesn't fit in with the bland majority is at least one spark of originality or strength that needs to be identified and nurtured. I'll give you two more brief examples that might give you ideas to use in your own search for the hidden outsider advantages you or a loved one can tap into.

THE MAN WHO SAW WHAT OTHERS MISSED

When Brian first came to my office for counseling, he had been laid off from his job and dumped by his girlfriend, who loved his humor, creativity, and warmth but called him "lazy" and "unfocused."

"I've been called that all my life," Brian told me. "My parents were both highly educated and had no patience with the fact that I found high school and college boring and frustrating. My older brother became a proctologist with fancy-ass patients in Beverly Hills and my younger sister is amazing at selling those million-dollar fixer-uppers that people have been buying lately. So whenever the family gets together, I'm obviously viewed as the defective one."

What no one in his family or his large impersonal schools had ever taken seriously was that Brian, like many creative and easily distracted individuals, had a different kind of gift than the typical requirement of memorizing lists and repeating back lectures, two tasks that are highly rewarded in over-filled classrooms. He might have been called lazy and unfocused— sometimes even "stupid"—but in fact he was intelligent and innovative in specific untapped areas.

I got my first glimpse of Brian's highly specialized brilliance during our second therapy session when we were talking about a film that Brian had seen the previous weekend, which I'd seen with my wife two weeks earlier. Whereas I had been moved by the character development and the psychological themes of the film (I'm a therapist, go figure), Brian had been fascinated by the visuals, the props, the set design, and the lighting—things that I had barely noticed and that I knew little about.

He spoke eloquently in my office about the importance of historical accuracy and the inaccuracy in the art direction of that film. He knew exactly which camera angles and lighting techniques had added to or detracted from the look of each scene. This man who had been called "unfocused" by his teachers, parents, siblings, and ex-girlfriend was clearly gifted when it came to taking in the rapid-fire visuals of a motion picture and appreciating their most subtle intricacies. After listening for a few minutes to his insights into the aesthetics of the film, I said, "Wow! You've got the makings of a whole new career direction. But it's going to take some time and effort."

That was the beginning of a breakthrough for Brian. He had been struggling at various jobs that didn't fit his skills or his passion. Now he began to explore in a systematic way the possibility of a career in props, set design, lighting, and art direction for films, television, and music videos. Each week in therapy, we talked about his concerns and what specific steps he could take in the next few days to get closer to his dream.

For example, I suggested that Brian initiate at least one phone call or lunch conversation each week with people he knew who were already making a good living in these fields in order to find out the hurdles, the requirements, and the intricacies he'd face. I also recommended that Brian begin to keep a daily journal of his ideas about props, lighting, and set design and his contacts with people in the business. And he signed up for two adult education classes that were hands-on and creative, unlike the boring lecture and memorization classes he had struggled with years ago.

In addition, we began to address the lifelong focusing and persistence issues that had stopped Brian in the past. Like most creative individuals, Brian had great ideas but usually not enough follow-through. I asked him to read and report back to me about a few excellent books on how to refocus each day and deal effectively with distractibility. (See the recommendations in the Sources section at the back of this book for specific suggestions). I also asked him to consult with an expert on medications designed for focusing problems, as well as an expert on biofeedback, to learn about some options that might help him follow through on his good ideas more consistently.

Despite his previous reputation of being "lazy," Brian took each of these recommendations to heart, and within a few months we began to see progress. Five months into his counseling, he told me, "I'm finally understanding what my brain is good at and how to use it to maximum effectiveness. I just wish I'd known this stuff years ago so I could stop trying to pretend I fit in at jobs where I was completely in the wrong place doing the wrong things."

Twelve months after his first counseling session, Brian was starting to get a few jobs in his new field. At some of his first jobs he was underpaid and overworked, but he soon began impressing some well-known producers and directors, who hired him back for more and more lucrative projects.

After two years of focusing on his strengths and keeping up the weekly phone calls and lunches with people who share his passion for film visuals, and journal writing, Brian has become a respected and sought-after prop master and set designer with a terrific highlights reel of his innovative solutions to tough production dilemmas. He has been nominated for an award for one of his projects, a music video, and it's opened up new contacts and job offers for him. You've probably seen some of his work, but you won't have noticed the hundreds of hours and subtle aesthetic decisions that went into finding and designing the right look for each scene. That's because Brian makes it look seamless.

After Brian completed his counseling sessions, I didn't hear from him for six months. But then I ran into him at a movie theater near my office. Brian told me that his career is still going well and his personal life has gotten much better. "My new girlfriend and I have been together for almost eight months," he said. "She absolutely understands my issues about being easily distracted and what it takes for me to stay on track. Unlike my family, my early bosses, and so many others who didn't get who I am, she knows that I've got a great future as long as I stick to the refocusing skills I've learned the past couple of years. We're very much in love and when I proposed to her on her birthday a few days ago, she said yes."

THE WOMAN WITH THE PEAR-SHAPED GENES

My client Rebecca grew up in a family where her younger sisters got the skinny genes from their stunning mom and she got the pear-shaped DNA from her father's side. For years she battled with diets, diet pills, exercise programs, depression medications, and numerous psychotherapies to deal with her feelings of self-consciousness. It didn't help that Rebecca's two closest friends from college became fashion models. As Rebecca describes it, "When I would walk into a room with my younger sisters or with my college friends, you could see the eyes of every male and female racing past me to get a long look at the stunners next to me. I always felt like saying, 'Stop staring and take a photograph. It'll last longer.'"

Rebecca had always been interested in clothing design; when I met her, she was working as a hired shopper for a drama series on network television. Each week it was her job to go find the right outfits for a notoriously difficult actress on the show who was so thin you worried if she had enough to eat. As Rebecca explained, "It's quite embarrassing to walk into a store and start browsing in the section for petite figures when every salesperson on the floor can see I would never fit into any of these outfits in my wildest dreams. In addition, I often feel that much more pear-shaped and heavy because of living in a city where very few women have a realistic body type. I'm surrounded at work each day by women who haven't had anything but a salad recently—or they're secret bingers who frequently need to 'give back' their lunch. Oh, the joys of trying to fit in at a Hollywood studio set."

I wanted to help Rebecca deal with her lifelong sense of being an unwelcome outsider in the high-pressure world of super-slim women. But since I'm no expert on clothes (and as I said earlier, I don't have much of an eye for design), I wasn't sure what to say that might be helpful.

Yet in our therapy sessions each week, I kept noticing that Rebecca always walked in wearing some extremely creative combination of clothes that seemed to have the right colors, shapes, cuts, and design elements to accentuate her own good looks. So on a day when she was again describing to me her painful self-consciousness about her pear-shaped body, I took a risk and asked her, "Has anyone ever told you that you have an amazing talent for putting together outfits for yourself that truly work?"

Rebecca looked at me silently for a moment. I was worried that maybe I'd made a mistake in commenting on her physical appearance, which was such a sensitive topic for her. But then she smiled and said, "No, as a matter of fact I've always been told I should specialize in designing outfits for women who are half my size. I've never been encouraged to come up with outfits for women who have my kind of figure."

That was the start of a new direction in Rebecca's career. Instead of feeling ashamed or unacceptable for having what she knew to be "a realistic body type," she started to treat it as an advantage. Over the next several months, Rebecca began to develop her own line of outfits that made pear-shaped women look great. While she held on to her day job for a while to help pay the bills, she eventually got out of the business of shopping for super-thin actresses. With money borrowed from two of her friends and an eccentric aunt who also came from the full-hipped side of the family, Rebecca began setting up showrooms and putting together portfolios to sell exquisite looks for "realistic" bodies like her own.

This change in attitude not only made Rebecca a lot of money over the next several years, it also made a huge impact on the way she felt about her own looks and her own sensuality. Like many people who have lost sight of their own beauty because they are constantly comparing themselves with unrealistic images in the media, Rebecca was finally learning how to invite herself back into the circle of people who belong. The day she completed her therapy, she told me, "I had always felt like someone who didn't have a chance to be appreciated or loved because I've got the wrong genes and the wrong body type. But something shifted inside my brain and it's made me start to appreciate not only my own good looks but the beauty of so many women who get overlooked in our society."

The next time you are in a store and you see a brilliantly designed outfit that makes a pear-shaped body look beautiful, there is a good chance you are seeing one of Rebecca's designs. I hope her story will cause you or someone you are advising to ask, "What if instead of believing there is something wrong with the cards I was dealt, I can begin to appreciate and do great things with exactly what's been given to me?" It's not easy to do, especially if you have spent a lifetime feeling "one down" from someone else who was dealt a more socially acceptable hand. But for Rebecca and for so many others I have counseled—and perhaps for you—this change in perspective can bring success and tremendous joy.

Benefit #3: Having a Reputation as an Outsider Gives You the Freedom to Speak Your Truth and Do What Matters, Whether It Makes a Lot of Money or Not

In case you haven't noticed, we live in a society that puts a monetary value on everything. That's why many people who are pursuing a goal that doesn't bring in immediate and substantial dollars sometimes feel like outsiders because everyone around them is so focused on quick returns. But I was fortunate enough, during my very first job after receiving my master's degree in 1976, to meet a courageous man who taught me something valuable about what really matters in life.

THE PERCEPTIVE LONER WHO TOOK A RISK

I was working in the research department of Doubleday and Company in New York doing market research projects and serving as an internal consultant for Doubleday hardcovers, Dell paperbacks, the Literary Guild book clubs, and the new alternative media ventures of the corporation.

One afternoon the phone rang in my office and I was asked to attend a meeting with an author whose long-delayed book was about to come out from Doubleday. The man's name was Alex Haley. The book was called *Roots*.

He was born in Ithaca, New York, when both of his parents were in graduate school. He grew up in Henning, Tennessee, where he heard stories from his grandmother and several aunts about his ancestors in Africa, including one particular man named Kunta Kinte.

An insightful loner who liked to wander and explore, Alex Haley worked for many years in the Coast Guard, traveling around the world on large ocean vessels where he learned first-hand about various cultures. As an American of African heritage, Haley often felt like an outsider in the mostly Caucasian Coast Guard crews and in many of the ports where they called. In addition, as a serious and introspective thinker, he felt like a bit of an oddball among his Coast Guard colleagues, most of whom were far less cerebral.

But the solid pay and the sense of adventure kept Alex in the Coast Guard for many years until he finally decided to risk trying to become a professional writer. At first, his efforts to get published resulted in a seemingly endless stream of rejection letters and financial hardships. At one point he lived in a basement apartment in Greenwich Village with almost no money. "I was prepared to starve," he said. "I only had eighteen cents left and a couple cans of sardines and that was it."

But he kept coming up with ideas for articles and people he wanted to interview. After several years of frustration and hardship, Haley did get a few paychecks from tracking down, interviewing, and publishing articles about several prominent figures, including Martin Luther King, Jr., Miles Davis, and Malcolm X.

Haley's curiosity and strong sense of integrity were so compelling that he was asked by a small publisher to co-author *The Autobiography of Malcolm X*, which was not an easy project because of how tense things were during the final few years of Malcolm X's short life. However, the well-written book caught the eye of a few editors at mainstream publishing houses. It was suggested to him that he should write other celebrity biographies that might bring in substantial dollars. But Haley had a personal project that mattered to him deeply and for which he was willing to forgo the money. He signed a contract for just $16,000 with Doubleday to write a book based on the stories he had heard as a child about his ancestor Kunta Kinte from Gambia on the west coast of Africa.

The small up-front payment from Doubleday lasted barely a few months; the manuscript was due only a few months later. But Alex wasn't ready yet to hand it in. Instead, he went on meticulously researching the elusive connections between his grandmother's life in Henning, Tennessee, and his ancestor's life in West Africa for almost twelve years. He kept explaining to his editor and the publishing executives that this personal quest—to discover what really happened after Kunta Kinte was captured and put into a slave ship—had to be told right. Over and over they gave him a six-month extension of the deadline. After twelve years no one was sure if this had been a mistake or if there was ever going to be a book at all.

At one point during the exhausting weeks, months, and years of searching for the missing information that would finally connect his ancestors with his own life, Haley found himself completely stumped and unable to keep going. I remember watching the pain in his face as he described lying face down on a plank of wood on an old slave ship he was researching and saying to himself, "This entire quest of mine is going nowhere. There's no way I'm ever going to make this complicated story come together. Besides, who's going to be interested anyway?"

During that moment, he recalled feeling connected to the spirit of one of the mistreated, heroic ancestors he had been learning about in his family tree. In a soft voice, Haley explained, "It was at that moment I realized I couldn't give up. For reasons I will never fully understand, I felt strengthened by the courage and the pain of these deeply human ancestors who were cut off from their loved ones, taken away in chains, and yet their souls are still connected to my own soul."

At the business meeting where I first met Alex Haley, there was a disagreement brewing about whether *Roots* would appeal only to a black audience or would draw in readers from all races and ethnicities. I remember Haley looking around at the room filled with marketing and business managers, all of whom were white. He leaned forward with that compelling expression of his. "There are two things that I keep in mind and that help me stay true to who I am. The first is that I am not a slave to money. I do what I do because that's exactly what my soul is telling me I need to be exploring and learning."

You have to understand that in the modern world of publishing, you don't often hear someone saying he doesn't care about money. It was completely silent now in the meeting room. Then the silence was broken by Haley's slow but deliberate speech. He said:

"The second thing that helps me keep my sanity is that I believe if you tell the truth and you do it with grace and respect for the person who is hearing your truth, some amazing things can happen. Just like the Bible says 'the truth shall set you free,' so have I found that there is a mysterious power in seeking the truth, speaking the truth, and risking everything for the truth. Living that way brings me more joy than focusing on dollars or the approval of others."

When he stopped talking, there was silence again. But his passionate words have stuck in my head ever since. I'll admit I worry about financial security as much as the next person. But I also began to consider the freedom and the personal integrity I saw in Alex Haley. It made me wonder if it's possible that "seeking the truth and speaking the truth" can eventually help us as human beings, on a personal level and in society as well. What would it mean to have a stronger sense of truth in our daily interactions, our business dealings, our government policies, and our connection to other people and the living things of this world?

I have a sense that Alex Haley would have been enormously pleased if his book didn't make much money but simply uncovered the human reality of what happened to his ancestors. Ironically, the finished book, entitled *Roots: The Saga of an American Family*, became one of the most successful projects in publishing history, with enormous worldwide book sales and one of the highest-ever television ratings when it was turned into a miniseries on ABC.

For the rest of his life, Alex Haley was invited to speak his truth to thousands of groups, large and small, from all backgrounds around the world. In front of one captivated audience after another, he talked about the importance of each human being's personal quest to find out where we come from and how, regardless of race or ethnicity, our family struggles, disappointments, and triumphs over many generations still impact our choices in life.

So let me ask you a question, dear reader. Are there some areas in your life where you have been reluctant to be truthful with someone who you fear will misunderstand you, judge you, or reject you? Are there some issues about which you are not always truthful with yourself, but slip into denial or rationalizations? Is there a creative project or personal quest that requires more of your courage, honesty, and commitment to complete?

If, like Alex Haley, you are already an outsider to some extent and you're willing to admit it to yourself and to others, this can give you the freedom to take an extra step into being more authentic and more courageous in all areas of your life. Instead of being driven by a fear of someone finding out you are "different," you can face the fact that you'll never be a blandly normal insider. Once you fully accept your outsiderness, you'll find there's a lot less holding you back from your true calling. Stepping boldly across the line to being "unconventional"—or no longer trapped within the bounds of what most consider normal these days—energizes you to start waking up each day with much less fear and far more vitality.

I wish you could have been in that room on the 43rd floor of 245 Park Avenue to see for yourself how Alex Haley spoke from the heart in front of a bunch of light-skinned men in very dark suits. I hope that the next time you are outnumbered or surrounded by people who don't share your values, you take a deep breath and say to yourself, "They already believe I don't fit in. What do I have to lose?"

Benefit #4: If You've Been Rejected or Isolated in the Past, You Can Appreciate More Deeply the Importance of Loving and Being Loved

The fourth and final benefit I will discuss in this chapter is the most personal. It's about the human longing to connect and be loved. In so many families and relationships, connection doesn't happen very smoothly.

Yet I've found that men and women who have felt the pain of losing a loved one, or who have known the frustration of being currently alone in the world of coupled-up pairs, tend to have an extra-strong appreciation for the importance of truly connecting with another human being. The better you know the feelings of severe loss or isolation, the better you can understand the exquisiteness of finding someone who cares deeply and who comes through with genuine warmth.

For example, there's a wonderful book called *Motherless Daughters,* by a researcher and writer named Hope Edelman who lost her mother at a young age, which explores in detail the isolation and the possible strength that comes from dealing with the painful loss of someone you cherished. My older sister, Janice, and I have read Edelman's book from cover to cover, because our own mom died after a four-year battle with cancer when I was fourteen and Janice was seventeen. Edelman captures beautifully the longing for love that grows even stronger when you've been tossed into a parallel universe as a result of losing a parent, sibling, or close friend early in your life.

I remember vividly the sense of isolation I felt for many months when I couldn't sleep night after night in junior high because I knew my mom was dying. Each day in school I felt like a complete outsider, because even as the teachers and other students were talking about homework assignments and school activities, my mind was elsewhere, wondering if my mother would ever see the inside of our home again. I didn't have the words to describe what I was going through. That enormous sense of loss and aloneness is something I can't forget, yet it makes each moment in my adult life with my wife, Linda, and my son, Steven, all the more precious. Every time I comfort my son in the middle of the night or wake up next to my wife in the morning, I feel all the more gratitude and joy because I know what it's like to watch helplessly as someone slips away.

WHAT ARE YOUR OWN PAINFUL LOSSES?

The death of a loved one isn't the only form this sense of loss can take. That intense unmet longing for love can grow in anyone who has felt isolated or set apart—perhaps as a result of coping with his parents' divorce or with a painful breakup in her own adult life. In my therapy practice, I have been amazed at how many men and women from all walks of life describe feeling like helpless outsiders when their parents fought, or when mom and dad finally split up, or when their own cherished relationships fell apart.

To watch an important romantic bond being severed right in front of you—whether it's someone else's or your own—leaves its mark deep. If you have experienced firsthand the pain of divorce and the isolation and ostracism that often follow, you are likely to have an extra appreciation and longing for the richness of a love that lasts. Many men and women spend their entire adult lives learning how to rebuild the sense of security and trust that was shattered when they saw a precious but fragile relationship fall apart. But when they do find love again, it's all the more exquisite because they know how fragile love can be.

Or you might have an outsider's intense appreciation and longing for love because you were never able to get a particular person—a parent, friend, or romantic partner—to say those three key words: "I love you." You pretend you can get by fine without this person's approval or words of appreciation. But in your heart you know it hurts to be cut off or shut out from someone with whom you deeply want to connect. And this longing can translate into an even sweeter sense of delight and inner peace when someone important to you finally gives you a sign that he or she does care.

THE MAN WHO LONGED FOR HIS FATHER'S LOVE

Let's end this chapter with one true story of the outsider's quest for a break-through of the heart. It's the passionate story of a remarkable man who kept searching for a way to connect with a particular loved one whose heart seemed to be out of reach. I hope it will stir your own courage for reaching out to someone you love.

First, a bit of background: When I moved to Los Angeles twenty-nine years ago, after living in the Midwest and the Northeast, I was under the impression that it would be very exciting to meet in person some of the writers, actors, and directors whose films were so inspiring. But I learned—firsthand and from my clients' stories—that many of these people are unpleasant, self-absorbed, or superficial in real life. Sometimes it's hard to believe the contrast between the warm and profound person you think you're going to meet and the not-very-decent person you do meet.

So I'm glad to report that one filmmaker whose work is amazing on screen turns out to be a sincere and generous soul in real life as well. Three different people in my counseling practice have told me in detail how the director Ang Lee has come through for them and treated them with kindness and respect. He seems to be someone who lives with the same integrity in daily life that his films would lead you to expect.

Many people know Ang Lee as a maker of thought-provoking, artistic films that include *The Wedding Banquet, The Ice Storm, Lust Caution,* and *Crouching Tiger Hidden Dragon.* What most people don't know about him is that he spent many years trying unsuccessfully to connect with his own father. Long before he made his first film, Lee grew up in Taiwan as the eldest son of a highly disciplined and very well-respected school principal. Lee's father expected that the eldest son would follow him into the academic world to become a teacher first and then eventually a respected administrator himself. But Lee wasn't sure if he wanted to fit into his father's conventional life; he sensed he was drawn to art and theater, two fields that his family insisted would be a major mistake.

Ang Lee doesn't talk often about his private pain, but he explained to an interviewer he trusted, "I always felt like a disappointment in my father's eyes. There was a strong sense of family duty and I knew I was hurting my father by my failing to live up to what was expected of me. I couldn't even mention art or the entertainment business in our home. It would disappoint my father so enormously if I didn't follow his path. This made it hard to breathe, hard to face my true self."

In Taiwan there is an entrance examination for the national university where one would train to be a teacher. Despite his desire to please his father and not let him down, Ang Lee failed to score high enough on this crucial exam. It was a devastating moment for the family. He says, "For my generation, it was like death to disappoint your parent so completely."

Despite this enormous shame, Lee eventually enrolled in an art school, developed his interest in acting, and did a mandatory two-year stint in the Taiwanese army. Yet he was not optimistic about the possibility of working as an artist or an actor with his family nearby. So he decided to move to the United States and study acting at the University of Illinois.

But because he was a recent immigrant who had trouble speaking clear English (and he was auditioning against some extremely talented competition), Lee wasn't able to land very many roles. Once again he felt like a failure and he wasn't sure whether to stay in the United States or go back to Taiwan.

This bleak period led to many months of introspection and extensive reading in which he became interested in the history of film. Refusing to give up on his dream of expressing himself through art, Lee began to write and direct a small student film of his own.

This first film won an award from New York University, but it didn't pay the bills. Lee spent the next six years in what is known in the film business as "development hell": pitching projects to film producers, being told there is interest in your project, waiting for a green light, but coming up empty and disappointed in the end, over and over again. Every few months there would be a nibble on one of his ideas, but then the executive would pull the plug because there were so many hundreds of other projects to choose from. After six years of these near-misses and lots of unpaid bills as a result, Lee feared he would never find his way into the select group of filmmakers who can make a living from their art.

At this point, after so many failures and disappointments, most sensible human beings would quit pursuing the dream. Lee's career difficulties were compounded by the fact that they made the tension between him and his father even worse. He knew that he had let down his family and his family's sense of honor.

But after another period of introspection and the encouragement of a few friends, Ang Lee decided not to quit the film business. Instead, he wrote a very personal and heartfelt screenplay about a Taiwanese man whose complicated father comes to live with him in New York City. The script explores the estrangement between the father and the American-born daughter-in-law because of their cultural and language differences.

From the attempt to understand and connect with his own emotionally distant father, Ang Lee had written a very moving work of art. The script, entitled "Pushing Hands," was spot-on in its portrayal of the painful silences between human beings who want to connect but can't find a way. It eventually won an award from the Taiwanese government and was released as a low-budget art-house film that got excellent reviews in Asia and later in the United States.

Yet even while Ang Lee was receiving praise from critics and cultured audiences for his first few artistic but not very commercial films, he was still unable to win his father's approval. And he still felt like an outsider who didn't quite fit into the world of mainstream big-budget Hollywood. Nor did he feel as if he and his wife and kids fit into his father's traditional world in Taiwan.

This unpleasant sense of never quite fitting in kept Lee trying different ways to gain acceptance. He was offered many sensitive and artistic scripts to direct, but he kept saying no, because he was hoping someday to direct a huge commercial success that would prove he had finally "arrived."

That's why for several years he was afraid to risk directing a well-written (but probably not commercial) screenplay called "Brokeback Mountain," about two young ranch hands in backcountry Wyoming, that was offered to him by some talented screenwriters who loved his directing style. He chose instead to do *The Incredible Hulk*, a huge, expensive project filled with high-tech special effects that promised him the chance at a major box-office success and acclaim as a mainstream Hollywood director. If *The Incredible Hulk* succeeded, Lee hoped he would finally prove to his father and the world that he had made it.

Yet the complicated special effects problems and other expensive setbacks with the Hulk film became an ongoing nightmare. In 2003, after the film was finally completed, Ang Lee suffered a physical and emotional breakdown. His desperate attempt to achieve commercial success and acceptance by Hollywood standards was brutally slammed by the critics and did far less at the box office than expected. Feeling once again like a failure who didn't truly fit in anywhere, Lee was convinced it was time to get out of the film business altogether.

Like most outsiders who try to twist themselves into pretzels to fit in, Ang Lee felt empty and lost. Some people were advising him to get back to work quickly and find another commercial project that might at long last propel him into the select circle of highly paid studio directors. Others were suggesting it was impossible for an artist like him to maintain his personal integrity at a time when Hollywood was becoming obsessed with huge high-tech films and the pressure to achieve opening-weekend blowouts at the box office.

Emotionally and physically exhausted, Lee decided to make one more attempt to connect with his distant and disapproving father. He flew back to Taiwan and spent time reconnecting with where he'd come from and who he was as a child. He also found the courage to simply sit and be with his father.

During that visit, and for the first time in his adult life, Ang Lee took the risk of opening up to his father and telling him how lost and uncertain he felt. It was their most vulnerable heart-to-heart talk ever as the son admitted to his father, "I don't know if I can do this anymore." His father was quiet for a moment, and Lee feared that once again his disapproving parent, "who had never encouraged my film career even after I won several awards," was ashamed of his sensitive son.

But his father took a deep breath and told him, "You have to go on. You cannot quit." It was only a few words and a warm look of concern. But he felt his father's deep caring and admiration. In those precious moments and in the strong sense of shared love, Ang Lee received what he had been searching for all these years.

Lee flew back to the United States, wondering if he should direct another big-budget film or do something more personal. He was thinking again of the well-written script about the two young men in Wyoming whose love for each other had to be hidden. But could Ang Lee afford to say yes to a risky project with little chance of commercial success that might not even be allowed into chain theaters in the rural, conservative parts of the

United States? After the financial problems of *The Incredible Hulk*, was it career suicide to say yes to a project that had so many ways to fail?

Two weeks after returning to the United States, Ang Lee got a call to rush back to Taiwan. His father had died. After the funeral, the director who had spent his entire life knowing the pain of silently wanting someone's love decided to say yes and go forward with *Brokeback Mountain*.

According to Ang Lee, "When I thought about filming the scenes where Ennis and Jack have to face the fact that they can't express the complete love and freedom they want so strongly, it breaks my heart. It felt very personal and real. I began to sense that this would be a film that would speak to many people of every type. I knew that most of us would understand the same longing for love and true connection that these characters desire so passionately."

Many critics have said that the reason *Brokeback Mountain* became such an artistic and financial success was because of the painful silences, the unspoken longing, and the sense of artfully portrayed loss. Since Ang Lee had experienced a similar silence and sadness so many times in his own lifelong struggle to connect with his father, he knew better than almost anyone how to make each moment of pure human longing so compelling. His personal pain had been turned into a gift that touched millions of viewers.

At the Oscar ceremony in 2006, Ang Lee accepted the Academy Award for Best Director of a Motion Picture. He stood in front of hundreds of millions of viewers worldwide and thanked his father for his support and his love. Ang Lee had finally arrived.

A CONFESSION

So much of life remains a mystery. There was no course given in my training as a psychologist that explains why in this existence of ours, the experience of tremendous pain in one's life is often the prerequisite for tremendous joy. I do not claim to know why it takes an appreciation of loss in order to fully realize the miracle of being loved. I just know it seems to be a part of being human.

For Ang Lee and for thousands of other individuals I have counseled, the key issue is to not give up. Even if you are feeling estranged, isolated, or hopeless, there might still be the possibility of a moment of connection and warmth between you and the person you long to love and be loved by—or between you and the world that's been shutting you out.

You never know when the breakthrough will occur. All you can do is keep showing up with your integrity, your open heart, and your willingness to be surprised. Most of all, you must learn to trust that who you are at your very core is worthy of love. If you don't, you will probably keep trying to twist yourself into a pretzel.

Chapter Four

The Biggest Mistakes Most Outsiders Make

If this were simply a coffee-table book showing brief portraits of famous people who were once outsiders, I would give you ten or twenty uplifting stories next to a series of posed photographs of well-known people who didn't fit in at some point in their lives, but who later triumphed in a big way. This happy-ending format might be inspiring and comforting, but it would only be telling part of the story.

The more complete truth is that almost every person who has had the experience of being an outsider still struggles sometimes with insecurities left over from having felt the pain and frustration of not fitting in. It isn't easy for any human being to let go of painful memories of being left out, ignored, or isolated. I've found from extensive research with very famous, slightly famous, and not-at-all-famous people that most of us can barely remember what we had for lunch a few days ago, yet we vividly recall the exact details of slights and criticisms many years in the past.

What about you—can you remember what you had for lunch two days ago, nine days ago, or twenty days ago? How about a moment from your past when you felt verbally attacked or painfully ignored at work, in a social gathering, or at a family event? Can you picture the scene and feel the awkwardness almost as if it's happening once again?

According to brain imaging experts, these memories of being an outsider lodge in a few particular cells of your brain, almost like an unwanted Internet "cookie" that sticks to your hard drive (even if you had no intention of letting anyone store it there). The reason why this emotional "cookie" in your long-term memory is so important is that it can play tricks on your mind for the rest of your life. Years after a painful moment in which you felt like an outcast, a similar situation can come along and reactivate this remnant of emotion, with its feelings of being left out or vulnerable. Suddenly your entire identity and your sense of self-worth feel as if they are being challenged. And you may find yourself reacting—or overreacting—in some unfortunate and harmful ways.

So how do you get beyond the pain? How do you make sure the awkward moments from the past don't compromise your current well-being?

Let's be realistic about this: There is no plastic surgeon who can nip and tuck the insecurities from your long-term memory. But you *can* learn ways to respond more effectively when something in the present reactivates the pain of the past.

Please put your seat belt on, because we're about to go for a wild ride. In the pages ahead, you'll gain insight into the three common mistakes even the most logical individuals make when an adult situation retriggers a childhood or young-adulthood insecurity—and what you can do about it starting today. You'll meet a number of smart and sensible people like you who do some ungraceful, self-defeating things because of "emotional cookies" stuck on their cerebral hard drives. And you'll find tips on how to respond calmly and with confidence to these interruptive remnants from the past.

Mistake #1: The Chip on Your Shoulder

When you think of someone who "has a chip on his shoulder," who comes to mind? Is it someone at work who gets self-righteous and preachy over certain topics? Is it someone in your extended family who gets bent out of shape whenever she thinks someone isn't giving her enough attention or loyalty? Maybe it's someone in your social circle who can't let go of a frustrating incident that happened long ago, because it still clouds his vision and causes him to launch into tirades at bad drivers, slow clerks, or anyone else who doesn't respond the way he wants.

Or are you the one who tends to fly off the handle? Is there some incident from before the year 2000 for which frustration and resentments still linger in the back of your mind, making you overreact or get cranky at the most stressful moments? Is there some internal agitation that still keeps you a little too much on edge (and creates problems in your work or your personal relationships)?

THE ARTIST WE ALL THOUGHT WOULD MAKE HER MARK

There's a fine line between being creatively edgy in a good way and having a chip on your shoulder that causes you costly problems. For example, one of my closest friends in high school was a very talented and unconventional artist named Jill. Even at the age of seventeen, Jill's paintings, her pen-and-ink drawings, and her collages were original and beautifully done. Because of this, all of us who knew her in high school in Michigan assumed she would be recognized sooner or later as a major artist—or maybe as an art director or graphic designer—in New York or as part of some other important scene.

One of the most gripping things about Jill's art was its blunt honesty. Jill came from an extremely tense and competitive family in which her parents and siblings usually focused on status, conformity, and outward appearances, while she was all about shattering icons and breaking the rules. So her art had a terrific bust-your-chops quality of irony and surprise. A painting that looked at first like a happy scene of suburbia would quickly shift in your perception as soon as you noticed the daggers in the eyes of the family members and the dark crimson hues that were spreading ominously over the family portrait. Her art made you think and feel—her paintings and drawings would cause you to want to talk afterward about your strong reactions to each one.

But many years later, when I was living in New York, I ran into Jill at a restaurant in Greenwich Village and she told me that she had given up her art. As we talked for several hours that night, I saw the pain in her face and heard the sadness in her voice as she described how many times she had clashed with art teachers, gallery owners, managers, advisors, co-workers, and other potential allies who loved her art but couldn't deal with her sarcasm and her quick flashes of anger.

Like many multilayered people who've experienced a painful outsider upbringing, Jill had been given a blessing and a curse. The blessing was that her difficult family situation had helped to inject a powerful intensity into everything she imagined and created. The curse was that it had also given her an agitated impatience toward anyone who got close to her but didn't side with her 100 percent of the time.

I wish I could tell you that Jill worked through her agitation and found a way to thrive again as a talented artist. But in fact she got cancer and, after numerous chemotherapies, surgeries, and heartbreaking disappointments, died much too young.

At Jill's moving memorial service, one person after another spoke on the same theme: "If only Jill had been given more time to find a way to soften the chip on her shoulder. If only she had learned how to stop herself from being so reactive and pushing away those imperfect human beings who wanted to help her."

There was so much unfulfilled longing in Jill's creative soul, so much edgy brilliance that never got expressed and never reached the audiences that could have been moved by her insights. I think of her often, especially when I am counseling someone who has been given both the gift of being a rebel and the burden of being too volatile.

EXAMINING YOUR OWN SHOULDERS FOR CHIPS

Even though it's easy to see when someone else has a chip on his or her shoulder, it's much more challenging to recognize and admit what's going on in our own overreactions to daily stresses. When you look in the mirror before you go out into the world each day, you probably don't see right away that you might have a costly chip on your shoulder. What you probably see in the mirror is a sensible individual, far more "reasonable" and "rational" than most of the people you encounter on a daily basis.

But if we're going to be honest with ourselves, we might as well face the fact that most creative and unique human beings (including the most "reasonable" and "rational") have at least a few chips that need to be examined and managed effectively so that their old wounds don't sabotage their work goals, their family interactions, their personal relationships, or their physical health and well-being. So let's bring out a little bit of truth serum. Here's a quick exercise that I've found can move you rapidly out of obliviousness so that you can accurately and courageously deal with your own chips.

THE REWARD FOR SELF-KNOWLEDGE

Permit me to ask you a strange question that may be enormously helpful: What if you were offered a $10,000 reward for accurately describing at least one unresolved frustration or resentment that sometimes gets stirred up afresh? What would that particular chip of yours be? What is the lifelong insecurity or the unforgettable hurt from your past that makes you squirm inside or react to stressful situations with sarcasm, bitterness, or harsh comparisons of yourself to other people? What is the emotional wound, suffered long ago, that still flares up in subtle ways or causes you to shut down and go numb at the most unfortunate moments?

For just a few minutes, think about these specific clues to the barely visible chip you might be carrying:

- ✶ When you're in close proximity to a certain individual or group, do you tend to get quiet, act overly polite, or feel a bit insecure?
- ✶ When you're around a certain kind of person, do you tend to become impatient, short-tempered, or hostile in your thoughts and feelings?
- ✶ In what situations do you feel like a fish out of water, and what memories from long ago get stirred up?
- ✶ Around certain individuals or groups, do you find yourself comparing your lot in life with what these others have?
- ✶ What situations lead you to say or do things that you later wish you hadn't said or done?

My intention in asking you these very personal questions is not to cause you pain or make you feel self-critical. We've all got at least one chip on our shoulder—it's part of being human. My purpose in asking you to describe your own hidden chip is to help you learn how to deal with it more effectively so you don't make the same mistake that most outsiders make. Instead of shutting down or overreacting, what if you could be more aware, creative, and brilliant at those very moments when the chip on your shoulder is triggered?

THE ACTOR WHO HATED AUDITIONS

A few years ago I counseled an extremely gifted actor named Andrew who has done amazing work in live theater, television, and film. You may have seen some of his performances and been moved by them.

But Andrew lives with a secret frustration because he's smart enough to realize he has missed out on numerous callbacks and career opportunities as a result of a tiny but significant chip on his shoulder. For most of his adult working life, he has gotten rejected from many terrific roles he was extremely close to landing, because he just wasn't at his best during the tryout or the follow-up meetings.

During his first counseling session, Andrew told me, "I didn't want to come in for therapy. But my roommate thinks I'm shooting myself in the foot too often, especially at auditions and business meetings where I know the person sitting in front of me has the power to make a life-changing judgment about my own life. Whenever I'm face-to-face with a casting agent, a director, a producer, or some other big shot who has so much power over whether I get to work or whether I have to go back on unemployment, something happens inside me that I just can't seem to fix."

Andrew explained, "At most auditions and business meetings, I don't come across the way I want to come across. At these make-or-break moments, I'm pumped up and ready, but for some reason I can't seem to do my best work. Instead I start resenting just how powerless I feel around these people who are there to check me out and reject me like I'm a piece of meat in a supermarket."

When I asked Andrew if these feelings of powerlessness and resentment reminded him of any old hurts from his childhood and young adult years, he was silent for a moment, then said he wasn't sure what it might be about. So I gently asked him the question I just asked you: "If you were offered $10,000 to tell me a small chip on your shoulder related to these moments of being in a room with casting agents, producers, directors, and other actors, what might that chip be?"

In a flash, Andrew's face lit up. For $10,000 he could easily admit to the chip he'd been keeping secret for many years. (Like most of us, Andrew discovered that simply imagining an incentive could motivate him to unlock long-buried insights and memories.)

He said, "As a kid I felt powerless and resentful in school because most of the other students were being taken several times a week to acting classes, movement classes, music lessons, and other creative activities. I desperately wanted to do acting, dance, music, and improvisation classes, but my family couldn't afford these after-school programs or drive me all over town to study with the best teachers.

"You need to know that I grew up with a divorced mom who couldn't collect much financial support from my evasive dad, who was all talk and no follow-through. I resented that most of the other kids came from stable homes with more than enough money where they felt entitled to all sorts of good things in life. In my family, there was this sense of bitterness that we'd fallen off the success train and we had no clue how to get back on. Each night after school with my mom away at work, all I could do was watch old TV reruns and procrastinate on my home-work until my mom would come home and yell at me for being lazy and uncooperative."

I could see the frustration in Andrew's face as he described the sense of entitlement he resented in others and the sense of isolation he felt day after day as a teenager. I was beginning to understand why he felt agitated inside each time he was being judged or evaluated.

I asked Andrew, "When you're at an audition, a business meeting, an interview, or a social gathering—anywhere people are checking you out to see if they want to hire you for an important job—what runs through your head about the person in front of you who has the power to select you or reject you? Remember, if you were being given $10,000 to describe yourself, what would you say about the specifics of these resentments and insecurities?"

Andrew's face got tight and he stared at me for a moment with an angry expression. Then he said, "What do I feel when I'm at one of these high-pressure meetings? I feel pissed off. How did these stuck-up fools from their cushy backgrounds get so much power to be able to decide whether I'm going to be able to pay my mortgage or whether I'll have to take some crappy side job to pay the bills? Who made them God?"

Andrew was quiet for a moment, and then he spoke softly, in a somewhat embarrassed tone of voice, as he admitted, "I guess it's rather obvious why I don't seem to do my best work at tryouts and I don't come across well at these business meetings. I'm so pissed off inside that I lose all sense of what it means to be an actor who's focused on his craft."

TWO QUESTIONS TO REGAIN YOUR CLARITY AND STRENGTH

Like Andrew, have you ever been in a make-or-break situation at work, in a social clique, or at a family event where you looked around and felt frustrated that someone in a power position had so much clout to shape the ups and downs of your life? If so, here is a powerful technique that I've seen work well with many women and men who didn't want to let the chip on their shoulder cloud their vision or disrupt the make-or-break moment.

The first part of the exercise is playful. Imagine for a moment what outrageous thing you would say or do if you had permission to let the chip on your shoulder run the show. Instead of holding your breath and tensing up with the uncomfortable resentments or insecurities stirred up from long ago, this allows you to tap into your sense of humor and your sense of freedom.

I told Andrew, "For at least a few seconds before the meeting begins, or during a quiet moment, simply take a deep breath in and out as you ask yourself the first question: 'What would Chip do?'"

Andrew smiled as if I were kidding. "What would Chip do?" he said skeptically. "Is that what I'm supposed to ask myself?"

I looked him straight in the eye and said, "Yep, that's the question that can loosen you up and help you turn things around at these important meetings where you've tended to freeze up. Instead of holding your breath and tightening your jaw, I want you to take a deep breath in and out as you imagine what would happen if you let Mr. Chip have free rein. What bizarre, unfiltered action would you take, or what would you blurt out spontaneously, if you were letting the chip on your shoulder have complete uncensored freedom?"

I gave Andrew a few moments to silently imagine what Chip would do. Then I told him the second key question that he needed to ask himself to turn things around. "After a few seconds of letting your sense of humor and your sense of freedom run wild, take a slow, deep breath in and out as you ask: 'What would my strong, calm, centered big-picture self do?' Connecting with the 'big picture' is like looking at your life from a higher and more compassionate vantage point, and it's a powerful way to tap into a deeper wisdom and a profound inner strength that you will need if you want to bring out your best."

I could see Andrew's body language change as he began to imagine this second question in his mind's eye: "What would my strong, calm, centered big-picture self do?" It only took a few seconds for the tightness in his face and the tension in his body to turn into a powerful clarity and vitality.

From the perspective of brain biochemistry, these two opposing visualization questions have a remarkable ability to deactivate the anxious and angry part of the brain while strongly activating the creative, intuitive, and spiritually centered parts of the brain. In a matter of a few seconds, the anxious feeling in your body begins to unwind while your creativity and your inner strength get reenergized. After Andrew practiced this exercise twice in my office, he used it at a series of auditions and business meetings. Here's what happened:

According to Andrew, "At tryouts and face-to-face meetings with studio big shots, I'd always felt like a caged animal having to pretend to be nice when in fact I was resentful and upset inside. But when I did the first question of the exercise, asking myself silently 'What would Chip do?', I immediately felt a sense of freedom, playfulness, and release. For a few seconds I silently imagined letting off steam, telling this uptight, dorky producer sitting in front of me with all his arrogance and entitlement exactly what I thought of him.

"Then after a few seconds of feeling totally free and uninhibited, I took a couple of deep breaths in and out as I switched to the second question and asked myself, 'What would my strong, calm, centered big-picture self do?' Just saying those words and breathing slowly put me into the kind of centered calmness I sometimes attain after yoga, prayer, lovemaking, or a walk in nature. For the first time in years, I was clear, strong, and powerful during an important tryout. I not only came across magnificently to the producer, the casting agent, and the director, but I got the part. I'm happy to say my mortgage is now paid in full for several months."

I cannot guarantee that this "Two Questions" exercise will succeed all the time and get you everything your heart desires. Nor am I suggesting that the "emotional cookies" will disappear from your long-term memory and never flare up again. But I can say from experience that this exercise and its carefully worded questions will most likely improve your mental alertness and your creative brilliance at the moments when you need clarity the most. Instead of letting the chip on your shoulder drive your behavior and cause problems again and again, this quick exercise can help you bring out your best qualities rather than your worst overreactions.

Mistake #2: The Inability to See that Your Journey Is Sufficiently Viable

The second widespread problem for most creative and vulnerable outsiders is that someone else's life often looks so much better than your own. This is not just the common wish to have the better figure, bigger bank account, greater success, or nicer home of someone who seems to be having an easier ride through life. It's a much more profound devaluing of who you are and what your life is about.

This sense of devaluing yourself and wishing you could be more like someone else can happen to even the most thoughtful, spiritual, and compassionate individuals. One of my favorite stories from Jewish teachings is about a well respected but very human rabbi in Eastern Europe named Reb Zusya who has a dream one night in which he talks with the mysterious Divine Presence. He says, "At the end of my life, I suspect I will stand before You and be asked, 'Zusya, why couldn't you be more like Moses, the great teacher and courageous leader?'" Then he hears a gentle, mysterious whisper in response. "Zusya, my one and only Zusya: at the end of your life you will not be asked why you were not more like Moses. You will be asked why you were not more like Zusya."

HOW MUCH DO YOU SUFFER BY COMPARING?

Since most creative, original, or vulnerable human beings tend to get knocked off track when they compare themselves to others, please take a moment to examine your own habit of envying someone else's style rather than honoring your own deeper wisdom. You might uncover some important insights about the pressure you have faced to redirect your own soul's journey and win the approval of certain other people who urged you to do things their way instead of what you knew from your own insights was a better way.

Here is a quick inventory you can take of your own tendency to get sidetracked from the deepest longings of your soul:

- When you were a young child, did you ever have the sense that your family felt impatient with you, as if your unique way of being was "wrong" or as if appreciating your uniqueness would require them to be more flexible than they were willing to be?
- As a child, did you have a sibling, cousin, friend, classmate, or neighbor who almost always captured more of the attention and praise than you did?
- Did you ever hear your parents or teachers say, "Why can't you be like so-and-so?" or "We don't have time for you now, because we need to focus on so-and-so, whose issues are so much more pressing than yours."
- Were you ever told, directly or indirectly, that your struggles or your needs were a burden or a bother?

As a therapist, I've found quite often that the most interesting and unconventional people tend to pick up a sense of being uncomfortable in their own skin during their early childhood. Maybe your parents and teachers were overstressed and unable to take the time to truly understand someone as complex as you. Or maybe your family was focused on another member who demanded more attention than you. Possibly there was favoritism going on in your school, your sports teams, your place of worship, or your club activities, giving you the sense that someone else's style was more acceptable to the powerful insiders than yours. Or maybe you kept finding yourself in groups of competitive kids where certain dominant personality types grabbed most of the energy, leaving the rest of you to feel like neglected outsiders.

If you flash back in your memory to junior high and high school, can you recall how unbalanced the priorities and hierarchies were? Maybe, as in many adolescent social situations, there was a lot of attention given to the small percentage of highly coordinated, extremely competitive boys who made the varsity sports teams or the small percentage of highly compliant, quite extroverted girls who got selected for cheerleading or homecoming court, while the differing needs and talents of hundreds of other students were overlooked.

Or did the attention at your school go to the richest kids who had the best cars, clothes, and electronic gadgets, with everyone else feeling one down by comparison? Or did the praise and focus go to the narrow clique of genetically stunning kids who learned at an early age to get by on appearances, while the rest of the school felt unsure about their own looks? Did the same few kids at your school or after-school activities dominate social situations, prestigious clubs, and awards ceremonies year after year, leaving the rest to wonder, "Where do I fit in? When will it be my time to shine?"

THE PRESSURE OF SUCCESS STORIES

As an adult, you may be facing a whole new set of comparisons that can cause you to devalue your own life's journey and wish you had someone else's circumstances. For example, is there someone in your extended family who's enjoying good luck or quick success in areas where you have been struggling? Does that person have more money, more valuable real estate, fancier dinner parties, a more attractive spouse, nicer vacations, or better-behaved kids? At family events, do you find yourself losing sight of your own progress in life because you don't measure up to this other person's skyrocketing successes?

Is there someone in your organization or your industry who tends to get much faster promotions, raises, financial successes, creative acclaim, or smooth sailing on projects than you do? Do you sometimes feel disillusioned about your own modest achievements because you aren't getting the same glamorous fast-track results?

When you turn on the television, pick up a magazine, or read a newspaper, does your focus go straight to the outrageous triumphs of "celebrity superstars" and make you feel small by comparison? Or are you constantly bombarded by hyped-up stories of someone who has just "made a killing" in the field where you have been working very hard to eke out some gradual, one-day-at-a-time progress?

This tendency to compare yourself to someone who seems to be above you on some arbitrary pecking order can drain your enthusiasm and distract you from your truly important quests, especially if you have a self-critical mind that habitually and painfully compares your most stressful days with this other person's best or easiest days. These unfair contrasts can dramatically hamper your physical health and your emotional well-being.

In order to stay sane and healthy as a unique, creative individual, you may need to let go of the harmful pressure that says you must make a quick killing or defeat all your competitors. You may need to stop devaluing your own worthwhile journey in life and start finding a way to honor it and enjoy it more.

REDEFINING WHAT IT MEANS TO BE A WINNER

In the past few years, I've noticed that more and more of my clients feel as if they aren't able to keep up with the escalating time pressures and financial demands of modern life. As a result, they have a gnawing fear of losing ground in their fields or in their social circles. Each year there seem to be fewer people who feel as if they are "winning" at the game of life, while more men and women confide to me their concerns that they and their families are slipping farther and farther behind.

That's why it was so refreshing in the summer of 2006 when an unusual film called *Little Miss Sunshine* came along and poked fun at the win-the-quick-payoff sickness that has been spreading in our society. This quirky comedy—something of an "outsider" itself—had a low budget, no major stars, and a more intelligent script than most mainstream films. The project got rejected for several years before finally being rescued by a risk-taking investor who put up most of the funds. No distribution company wanted to touch this offbeat film at first, but then it began to win awards at film festivals. Eventually it opened to passionate reviews from a few critics and generated strong word of mouth in its early weeks.

According to one early review in the *Los Angeles Times*, *Little Miss Sunshine* hilariously punctures the grotesque bubble of the competitive American spirit in which 'winners' are recognized by their rigorous ability to conform to the standards imposed by the market and 'losers' include anyone who won't bow to its mighty will."

Essentially, what happens in *Little Miss Sunshine* is that an eccentric American family finds itself being torn apart emotionally by the unrelenting pressure to be "number one" in a world where diversity and uniqueness are constantly undervalued. The father, played by Greg Kinnear, is an unsuccessful motivational coach who desperately longs to fit in and has nearly lost his soul and originality in the process. In the desperate struggle to be perceived as "winners" in a world gone mad with bizarre childhood beauty contests and vicious backbiting between peers in various professions, this family is choking on the fumes of modern life.

But then, slowly and carefully, they begin to work together in honoring the off-center uniqueness that each of them has been given as a birthright. By the end of the film, they are no longer at each other's throats. Instead, they have found a way to give one another genuine love and strength for facing a frequently hostile world.

This highly intelligent film reminded me of the struggle that so many creative and soulful individuals face to keep their spirits strong in a world deadened by conformity and compromised by tacky bottom-feeders. I remember sitting in the crowded movie theater laughing and crying as I thought about several of my clients, especially an unforgettable woman named Cara, whose story may help you think in a new way about your own personal journey.

THE WOMAN WHO DIDN'T FIT INTO ANY OF THE BOXES

I first met Cara when she made a counseling appointment during her troubled junior year of college. She had been raised by ambitious immigrant parents who wanted her to go to medical school like her older sister, Jane. According to Cara, "My parents had worked long hours to give us the chance to fulfill their dreams of their two kids being affluent doctors. It didn't matter if those were our dreams or not. We knew not to let our parents down."

In high school Cara had begun to feel like an alienated outsider, not only because she was in an ethnic minority at her school but also because, as she put it humorously in my office, "I wasn't geeky enough to be accepted by the science geeks. I wasn't athletic enough to be one of the talented volleyball or basketball players who were the power elite at my school. Nor was I manipulative enough to be able to understand the constant game-playing of the most popular kids at my school. I wasn't even druggy enough to fit in with the stoners who hung out together on the fringes of the playground at recess."

Rather than let her hard-working parents down, after high school Cara agreed to attend a large university and take pre-med courses including biochemistry, calculus, and genetics, following in the footsteps of her brilliant older sister, who had been accepted at several top medical schools. Cara was also highly intelligent in many ways, but she was struggling to stay afloat in her pre-med program. Not only was she having sleep problems, stomach problems, and anxiety symptoms, she was also feeling spiritually broken because she didn't have time for her friends and she hated the nature of her work—the huge amounts of what she called "memorizing and regurgitating thousands of disembodied facts each week." She also told me she felt sick inside each time she was asked to cut up a delicate frog, a beautiful cat, or a lonely human cadaver while surrounded by fiercely competitive fellow students who seemed totally cut off from their feelings. "They were truly ready to become the next generation of narcissistic surgeons who could take command in an operating room someday but would never be emotionally available to loved ones or to their children."

A week before she called me, Cara had gotten drunk at a fraternity party and woken up the following morning next to a man she neither liked nor wanted to see again. As she told me the story of her night of "losing it," I could see the sadness in Cara's eyes, especially when she described the embarrassment of trying to find her clothes and wanting desperately to run out of that popular frat boy's dorm room.

Near the end of her first counseling session, I asked Cara an open-ended question that I sometimes offer to decent and caring men and women who have gotten thrown off track by the pressure they feel to be people they are not. I said gently to Cara, "In this first session, you've taught me a lot about how uncomfortable it is for you to feel like an outsider in your pre-med program. But what I don't know yet is whether life has given you any clues as to what your soul truly longs to do. For instance, is there some unforgettable moment in your life up to this point where you felt fully curious, fully alive, and fully engaged in something meaningful? Teach me what clues you've received so far as to who you really want to be."

Cara looked at me and her eyes filled with tears. "If you want me to describe a moment when I felt fully curious, fully alive, and fully engaged in something meaningful," she said, "what comes to mind is an experience I had in high school. My neighbor was in a wheelchair and I spent several months helping her out. I remember wondering what it must be like to have to navigate life when your legs don't work very well and the whole world, from crossing the street at a rushed traffic light to squeezing through a narrow grocery store aisle, is set up for people who aren't in chairs."

She continued, "Spending time with my neighbor made me very

curious and very concerned. I often think about how she's doing and what it must be like for her with each passing year."

Over the next several months, Cara began to explore the possibility of devoting her life not to the "affluent doctor" dream that her parents held so dearly, but to following through on her *own* dream of making life better for men and women who need to use wheelchairs and other assistive devices. In the next few semesters, Cara began taking a wider variety of courses and eventually developed a unique double major that explored the economics and management of nonprofit organizations along with the intricacies of social work, occupational therapy, and physical therapy. After she graduated, she went on to work part-time at several innovative agencies (including two that help ease the daily access and activities of people who cannot walk easily) and she completed a master's degree in nonprofit administration.

I am happy to report that Cara has become a highly successful leader in the growing field devoted to helping people who have physical challenges. Even though her parents and her older sister are still somewhat disappointed that Cara never became a "real success" by going to medical school, there are now hundreds of men and women whose lives have been dramatically improved as a result of Cara's innovative programs and leadership.

Like many people I have counseled, Cara walked in for her first counseling session with a sense that she was hopelessly falling behind her peers. She simply couldn't keep up with her highly motivated sister or her competitive peers in the pre-med courses. But once she was asked to explore her own soul's journey in life and to honor the experiences that she found deeply moving and meaningful, something shifted, and it showed in her emotions and her physical health. Cara no longer suffers from sleep problems, stomach problems, or intense feelings of anxiety.

I won't say her life is a picnic. Each year she faces complicated obstacles while trying to raise money for her nonprofit organization, and she has to be very creative to hold on to the best people, who are sometimes tempted to go work for more money elsewhere even though Cara has trained them exquisitely. But if you saw Cara's face today and compared it to the way she looked during her first counseling session, you would immediately see how much more alive and self-confident she is—and how much less frustrated and sad—than she was in the days when she was trying to be a copy of her older sister.

If you or someone you know has felt held back or discouraged because you're trying to live someone else's dream for your life, I urge you to begin the process of exploring what your own soul's journey may be. For Cara and many others, it begins with a direct question: "What gives me the strongest sense of curiosity, aliveness, and meaning?"

Even if you think it's too late to reconnect with your soul's deepest longings, I urge you to think again. I've seen many men and women—not only in their 20s and 30s, but also in their 40s, 50s, 60s, and 70s—benefit enormously from following through on a personal quest or lifelong curiosity that they'd pushed aside for many years.

It might be a volunteer activity, a part-time involvement, a full-time career commitment, or a brief adventure you've been putting off for far too long. Please take a moment now to ask yourself, "Is there something I need to explore while I still have the time and energy to make it happen? Is there some clue to my personal sense of meaning and purpose that life or God has given me already and that my soul needs to pursue?"

Mistake #3: The Tendency to Overcompensate—and Still Not Feel Like Enough

The third difficulty many people who have been outsiders face is never quite feeling fulfilled or at peace with their lives because, in order to make up for their earlier insecurities, they've set the bar so high. I've found that about half the people who felt left out or put down earlier in their lives try to overcompensate later by pushing themselves harder than a human being should be pushed.

Does that ring true for you or someone you care about? Are you under pressure to achieve a near-perfection that will somehow vindicate you or make up for the deficiencies and pain of the past? Maybe you've tried to compensate for the awkwardness of your earlier years by becoming extremely thin, enormously affluent, or highly articulate. Or maybe you've responded by not making waves, by making sure everything in your life is neat and tidy, or by obsessing over what gets the approval of your current circle of colleagues and friends. You may even have found a way to become an occasional insider in the very same group of people that once treated you like an outsider.

But there's probably a voice in the back of your mind that can cut right through any success you've achieved. It may say things like, "Who are you kidding? You know you're not really like the ones who were born into the right circles!" It may whisper, "Watch out! It's just a matter of time until the bubble bursts and everyone finds out who you truly are." It might be a murmur of insecurity: "It was a fluke that you got where you are today. You don't really deserve it." Or it may sound like a motor revving inside you, saying, "Don't let up for a moment. You better keep up the pace or you'll slip back into your old defective self."

THE GOOD LISTENER WHO MADE EVERYONE FEEL UNDERSTOOD

You can't always tell by looking at someone that he or she is living with this pressure, agitation, and fear of never being enough. For example, I once counseled a man named Jonathan who was gifted as a business consultant and executive coach. He was an incredible listener who could sit down with his consulting clients and truly understand their concerns, their goals, their struggles, and the steps that could improve their careers. If you saw Jonathan at work, you would see a man who appeared to have total confidence in choosing exactly the right words to be effective in any business situation.

Yet even though Jonathan was so successful in leading workshops for major companies and in consulting one-on-one with high-powered executives, he admitted to me during his first therapy session, "What no one knows about me is that deep inside there's an enormous amount of unhappiness and fear. There's a huge emptiness that I try very hard not to let anyone see. Even my wife and my kids don't know just how insecure I am underneath all this professionalism, competence, and empathy that I wear as a mask."

Jonathan had never been to a therapist before. But he'd been referred to me by his physician because he was beginning to suffer from severe stress, a short fuse, occasional heartburn, and other digestive problems as a result of his high-pressure involvements. I wanted to understand more about what he meant when he said, "There's a huge emptiness that I try very hard not to let anyone see." I have heard this feeling expressed by many of my clients over the years, but I've found it has a slightly different meaning for each. For some, it means they have considered suicide. For others, it simply means they feel occasional sadness or uncertainty. Still others feel emptiness deep inside because they have lost their sense of meaning and purpose in life. Finally, there are those whose "hollow feeling" comes from shame or guilt about something from their past that they have hidden away and that they work hard to make sure no one finds.

In Jonathan's case, I didn't get a clear answer when I asked him to describe what he meant by "a huge emptiness inside." He told me, somewhat evasively, "We all have some mystery about us, don't we, Doctor?"

I decided to wait a while before asking him for a more honest response. Some people who are in therapy for the first time, especially those who aren't used to the vulnerability it creates, need more time before they're willing to own up to what's truly going on.

But near the end of the first counseling session, as we were taking a thorough history of Jonathan's current symptoms, I happened to ask him whether any of his relatives had ever struggled with anxiety, depression, or a sense of emptiness. Jonathan didn't answer at first. His face had a blank stare for a moment, very different from his usual alert, charming way of relating.

I wondered if he had heard my question, so I asked it again. "Is there anyone in your extended family who has struggled with anxiety, depression, or a sense of emptiness?"

"I heard you the first time," Jonathan quickly replied.

Then he explained, "I don't think it's very important to what we're doing here. But I guess I should mention to you that I don't know much about my medical history because the fact is I'm adopted. I don't usually tell anyone about that part of my life. It's a long time ago."

I won't go into detail about Jonathan's complicated history. Suffice it to say that he'd been given up for adoption a few months after his birth and spent almost four years with three different foster families before eventually ending up with a very attentive set of adoptive parents. With that abrupt separation from his initial caregivers, his arrival in this life was neither smooth nor secure, and yet he had never shared his most intense secret feelings about it with anyone.

What I do want to explore with you is an aftereffect of early emotional trauma that I have seen repeatedly over the years from having counseled many adoptees, from studying with numerous experts on adoption, and also from being an adoptive parent myself. Research now reveals that when a person has felt abandoned or rejected early in life (because of either adoption or a variety of other early feelings of separation), that person may overcompensate later by trying to be "so good" or "so needed" that he or she won't get abandoned or rejected again. A child may also feel like something of an outsider living with different caregivers who are not related to him or her by blood—even if the caregivers are very loving and attentive—and will spend a lot of his or her life trying to figure out how to be irreplaceable or indispensable at work and in personal relationships. As one adoptee said of his family, echoing what dozens of others have told me, "I always felt I had to look extra hard for the signals and bend over backward to make these people stick by me no matter what."

WANTING EVERYTHING TO BE "CLEAN AND IN ITS PROPER PLACE"

Even if you're not an adoptee, you may have known the experience of feeling like a stranger in your family of origin, or you may have had early emotional trauma of another sort. Either way, this desire to overcompensate needs to be explored so that it doesn't run your life. You may want to ask yourself: Do you "bend over backward" in groups, work situations, or personal relationships so you won't get rejected? Do you feel pressure to prove that you somehow "belong"—that you are "irreplaceable"—because you sense that you don't easily fit in with your family, at work, or in social situations where there are "insiders" and "outsiders"? Do you ever worry that your romantic partner, your closest friends, or your colleagues won't stay with you through hard times if you don't somehow manage them or constantly anticipate their needs? Have you ever wondered why some people seem so relaxed and trusting that friendships and work relationships will turn out well, when you're always concerned about getting left out or rejected?

Sometimes the fear of being abandoned, and the pressure to be "so good" and "so needed" to keep another rejection or disruption from happening, can reveal itself in the smallest details of daily life. For example, many people from traumatic or unstable family situations find themselves obsessed with keeping order around the house. Or they feel, as Jonathan did, that they have to "take care of everything" and appear to be invincible for their spouses, their kids, or their co-workers in order to prove to them how irreplaceable they are.

These exhausting, unrelenting pressures to overcompensate are lurking under the surface in many hard-working and creative individuals who never seem quite satisfied or at peace with their own successes. You would be amazed at how many famous and admired men and women live with the fear that they aren't quite good enough and that they must keep everything in perfect order to justify their place in the world.

On the very same day that Jonathan came to my office and told me how "fanatically" he kept his car and his home clean and how he "went over-board" at times to "take care of everything" for his family, I happened to read in a magazine article that the singer Faith Hill (who was adopted at an early age by loving parents) calls herself "a neatness fanatic at home" and struggles with a self-imposed pressure to "do it all" for her loved ones. Faith Hill is well known for her physical beauty, for being a devoted wife and mom, and for having great success in her music career, and she has also started several charities (including one to help dyslexic individuals like her adoptive father, who struggled with reading). Yet despite all she has going for her, she admits she struggled with hidden emotional pain for many years as she tried to figure out where she came from. She says of herself, "I am a clean fanatic—I mean, really fanatic. Everything has to be clean and in its proper place."

This understandable human desire to make up for the painful and confusing moments of childhood by trying to be "perfect"—by making sure everything is "clean and in its proper place"—creates a pressure I have seen in all sorts of outsider individuals from a variety of backgrounds. If you have ever felt a twinge of fear that your history might come back to haunt you or that everything needs to appear "just right" in order to keep your world from falling apart, then you know this feeling all too well.

WHAT CAN BRING YOU THE INNER PEACE YOU NEED?

If you or someone you care about struggles with this recurring concern— "Am I good enough?" "Do I need to have everything in its proper place in order to be worthwhile?"—there is something you can do to reduce the anxiety. In my twenty-five years as a therapist, I have researched and tried out many different methods for helping men and women who have felt a recurring sense of emptiness, self-doubt, or inner turmoil, especially those whose perfectionism and high-pressure lives trigger physical symptoms such as heartburn, muscle tension, and sleep problems. My goal has been to find something effective and accessible that not only works well during a structured therapy session, but can help intelligent men and women in the midst of their stressful daily lives to break free of feeling "not quite good enough" and find a way to enjoy more inner peace.

What eventually helped Jonathan, as it has helped thousands of my counseling clients (from all backgrounds, adopted or not), is a spiritual technique that you can use no matter what your religious background might be, or even if you don't consider yourself spiritual or religious at all. It's an easy-to-follow method based on an ancient wisdom teaching that I've found can work wonders for overcoming feelings of emptiness and the pressure of perfectionism that so many people experience in their daily lives. Here's how it works.

THE DAILY RECENTERING METHOD

At a moment when you feel anxious or catch yourself doing something excessive to overcompensate for your imperfections, take a deep, relaxing breath in and out. Then put your right hand into your right-side pocket or the waistband of your clothing. Imagine that you take out a note and it reads:

You are a unique and amazing part of creation. You are an original. There is no other individual quite like you. You have nothing to apologize for. You have an amazing capacity for goodness, creativity, warmth, and wisdom. Don't forget who you are and don't stop looking for ways to express the positive gifts and insights you have been given.

Then take another deep, relaxing breath in and out and put your left hand into your left-side pocket or waistband. Imagine that you take out another note and it reads:

You are like a grain of sand. You can stop trying to be perfect. There is no pressure on you right now to be more than who you are already. You are part of a huge, ever-changing creative process that includes millions of grains of sand, strong swirling winds, and refreshing waves from the ocean that sometimes wash over and connect the sand particles. You don't have to figure it all out. You are an essential part of this vast universe that has many other good and caring individuals. Your job is not to carry more of the load than is necessary. You simply need to stay humble and calm about the fact that you are one of many.

The fascinating irony about each of us humans is that both of these notes contain the truth. We are all unique and amazing individuals who stand out from the crowd, and at the same time we are all humble grains of sand, just a tiny part of a vast universe of similar beings that can carry much of the load for us.

If you learn to breathe deeply in and out as you allow yourself to feel centered between these two extreme views—the "amazing individual" and the "humble grain of sand"—you will experience many moments of peace and sanity. Instead of feeling empty inside or constantly pressured to do more than is humanly possible, you can relax in the knowledge that you are part of an ever-changing universe of good and caring individuals. You can feel proud of your small and large accomplishments while at the same time feeling humble in the knowledge that this universe is a lot bigger and more interesting than you can ever imagine.

WHAT HAPPENS WHEN YOU TRY IT OUT?

I asked Jonathan to try this recentering technique at various stressful moments during his day. For example, he often felt rushed and tense at meals because he didn't want to slow down when there was so much important work to accomplish. So I asked him to stop before eating and slowly breathe a deep, relaxing inhale and exhale before reaching into each of his pockets to read the two notes.

Jonathan told me, "Taking just a few moments to breathe calmly and to see my role in life as both a unique individual and a humble speck of sand helped me slow down and unwind a bit before eating. I'm not sure why, but the combination of seeing myself as a true original, and at the same time admitting that I'm a small, nonflashy part of a limitless universe where others carry much of the load for me, took away a lot of the pressure that I carry around. In that moment of breathing deeply and holding those opposing notes in my right hand and my left hand, my early childhood experience of disconnection and abandonment didn't seem so significant and, as a result, overcompensating to prove I'm irreplaceable didn't seem so urgent. Remembering to be humble takes the pressure off and allows me to be just a good-enough human."

I also asked Jonathan to imagine these two notes whenever he was starting to feel stressed and emotionally distant toward his wife and his children. When he tried this out, he reported, "It seems to calm me down and make me a more creative and playful parent when I imagine myself to be both a unique original and a humble grain of sand. As soon as I took a deep breath and admitted that the whole world isn't resting on my shoulders alone, I lightened up a bit. When I envisioned myself as a grain of sand in a huge inclusive universe, it made me feel less obsessed with being perfect and this allowed me to just hang out, have fun, and be more fully present with my kids. That's something I haven't been able to do for many years."

This exercise has a similar effect on most people I've asked to try it. It allows them to relax and it keeps them from being so obsessively driven by their insecurities and their painful childhood memories. Maybe it's because our true identities are found between those two extremes—between having to prove who we are as unique, separate individuals and knowing that we are tiny parts of a vast connected universe. I hope it will work for you, as it has for so many others, and help you feel calm and centered at the moments when you are feeling pressured to overcompensate for who you are.

Chapter Five

Breaking Through at Work

If you feel like an outsider at work, what are your options? Where do you go for help when you feel as if some insider is making things difficult for you and impacting your livelihood? How do you deal with being pushed aside or mistreated by people motivated only by their own self-interest?

Several years ago, a cousin of mine went to see a prominent psychotherapist to discuss the problems she was having in her career. After two expensive sessions spent describing her frustrations about a dysfunctional corporate higher-up, my cousin asked the prominent therapist what she should do.

The therapist explained in a slow, deliberate, authoritarian voice, "This is what you must do. In order to be a whole person and not remain a victim, you must confront this corporate idiot and don't hold back. You must sit down face-to-face with this harmful person and tell him exactly how you feel."

My cousin did as the therapist suggested. She was fired a few weeks later, and she spent the next eleven months running up credit card debt while she looked for a new job. So much for advice about confronting the "corporate idiot" or becoming a "whole person."

What's Realistic?

Now let's get real about dealing effectively with the competitive games and difficult characters you face in the workplace. In this chapter, you will learn specific steps for making things better in your career, while at the same time protecting yourself against hasty or ill-advised actions that can make things worse.

First of all, I promise not to say things like "Go confront your boss or your top customer and tell him (or her) exactly how you feel." That's because before I completed my Ph.D. in psychology, I received a master's degree in management and worked for Doubleday and American Express, where I learned first-hand how to do well even if you don't fit the corporate mold. For more than twenty years, I have consulted for numerous innovative and unconventional leaders nationwide in both the profit and the nonprofit sectors. I have listened hard to find out from women and men in a variety of fields what gets results and what doesn't get results in stressful real-life situations.

Important Skills That Don't Come Naturally

The techniques in the pages ahead are especially beneficial for anyone who has felt like a fish out of water in a company, or any work interaction, where the controlling insiders baffled you with their way of doing business. There are specific skills and strategies that don't come naturally to most compassionate human beings, because often the norms of the workplace are established by the most self-absorbed and least empathic individuals.

So please don't beat yourself up for being blind-sided or outmaneuvered by people who play by a nasty set of rules. Just as the pecking order of popularity in high school is established by certain insensitive and narrow-minded folks, so are the unspoken rules in many aggressive companies often devised by certain hard-driving narcissists who think it's their way or the highway. As a result, you may find yourself at times dealing with power struggles so irrational and frustrating that you ask yourself, "Do I really belong here?"

For example, in the past few months or years, have you bumped up against one or more of the following workplace dilemmas?

✵ A person at work who deliberately cut you out of the loop so that he or she could get away with something that you would have opposed

✵ A situation in which you spoke up and it got you into trouble

✵ A company policy that made absolutely no sense but had to be followed anyway

✵ A boss, co-worker, colleague, or customer who was verbally abusive, but to whom no one could talk back because he or she had too much clout

✵ A creative idea that got shot down because someone important felt threatened by a change in the status quo

✵ A disappointment when colleagues you thought you could trust didn't back you up on a key decision because they didn't want to make waves

✵ A person at work whose incompetence, gossip, backbiting, or manipulation was tolerated because he or she was a family member, a flirtation partner, or a personal favorite of someone in power

Let's face it—there are subtle games of inclusion and exclusion that some people seem to know how to play instinctually and that other intelligent men and women find hard to understand even when they're exposed to these situations repeatedly. Here are some skills and steps that can increase your chances of staying sane, healthy, and successful in your work life, even if "office politics" is a game whose rules you can't quite follow:

Skill #1: See Each Unpleasant Interaction Not as a Personal Failing, but as a Workout for Getting Wiser

Most people secretly fear that there must be something wrong with them personally—and find that their self-worth is diminished—when they come up against a boss, co-worker, or customer who acts in a rude, manipulative, or verbally abusive manner. I agree that it hurts on many levels (emotionally, spiritually, financially) to be treated harshly at work. There's nothing quite as disheartening as getting dressed for a big day, showing up at an important meeting, and then being snapped at in a demeaning tone of voice by someone in a position of authority.

But what if you change the way you look at these challenging moments in your work life? What if you creatively imagine that you are in a fascinating and inspiring real-time workshop called "Advanced People Skills, Graduate Level" and that each stressful interaction is a beautifully crafted case study designed by a compassionate teacher to help you boost your strength and learn a crucial skill that will serve you well for many years?

This creative shift in perception is an especially important tool for you if you grew up in a situation where you felt picked on, excluded, isolated, or treated badly. If some unpleasant person at work does something that reminds you of the mistreatment you suffered as a child, it's natural to feel as if you are once again helpless, hopeless, trapped, or powerless.

But what if you were able to switch into inquisitive learner mode—"Advanced People Skills, Graduate Level"—and immediately say to yourself:

"This is going to be interesting! This situation may look ominous to the untrained eye, but I've traveled a long road to get where I am right now. I'm not going to let this abrasive person ruin my mood or destroy my self-worth. I'll bet there's a way to respond effectively to this dilemma, and I'm going to find it."

Then, instead of feeling like a helpless victim, you might find that you are suddenly open to the possibility of staying strong and professional.

What exactly does it mean to "respond effectively" to a situation at work where some powerful insider snaps at you in a demeaning way or keeps you out of the loop on an important decision? What is an effective approach to ugly personality clashes at work (one that won't get you fired or shunned)?

PICK DOOR NUMBER THREE

Most people who get treated badly by a difficult boss, co-worker, or customer quickly fall into the most common human reaction, which I'll call Door Number One. It consists of going back into your office or cubicle and feeling like crap. You're not sure what to say, so you say nothing. You're not sure what you can do without making things worse, so you do nothing. Maybe you numb out with sweets or carbs to quell the pain. As you can probably tell, I don't really recommend Door Number One (the Powerless and Defeated option) as a viable solution.

Then there's Door Number Two, which is the second most common human reaction to stressful workplace situations. It consists of opening your mouth before you've had a chance to think clearly and lashing out with sarcasm or a nasty remark toward the boss, co-worker, or customer who's getting under your skin.

Both of these unprofessional reactions usually create more problems than they solve. Shutting down in resentment often makes you look like a doormat inviting more mistreatment. Lashing out impulsively can cost you your job, jeopardize an important account, or lodge an unfortunate remark in everyone's memory that you'll never fully erase. As any basketball, hockey, or football fan knows, the player who gets thrown out of the game is usually the one who is seen hitting back, not the one whose cheap shot started the whole thing.

That's why you quickly need to pick Door Number Three—to find a strategy more competent and professional than just shutting down or becoming sarcastic. For an example of how to do this successfully, let me tell you about Krista, a soft-spoken and caring young woman who works for an extremely volatile boss in a highly competitive company in the financial services field.

"I WASN'T SURE WHETHER TO QUIT"

As Krista told me when she first came in for counseling, "My boss can be impossible at times. He micromanages and criticizes much of what I do. He yells and says obnoxious things whenever the pressure and deadlines get too intense for him. He calls me late at night and early in the morning to ask me to handle things he's too arrogant to handle by himself."

Why does Krista keep working with this difficult individual? She explained, "He's brilliant at how to grow a successful company and he's regarded by many people as the most respected executive in my field. When he isn't criticizing my work or screaming at me, he's actually been opening doors and making valuable connections for me that I couldn't make on my own. Plus I've got bills to pay, so I'm not ready yet to tell him what a jackass he is sometimes."

But Krista said she had been close to tears on the day when she decided to call and make her first appointment with me. In the middle of a meeting with several of Krista's colleagues in the room, her boss had yelled at her for almost twenty minutes about an important and lucrative deal that had unexpectedly gone to one of their rivals.

"My boss blamed the whole thing on me," Krista said, "and accused me of not doing enough to make the deal happen. On one level I know it wasn't really my fault, but somehow, after my boss ripped me a new one in front of my co-workers, I began to wonder if I should have done more to save this important deal."

She admitted, "There have been so many times in the past year when his booming voice and his patronizing attitude have made me feel as if I don't have what it takes to succeed in this field. I've studied and prepared for many years to reach this level of responsibility, but each time my boss goes ballistic or implies that he's frustrated with my performance, I wonder how long I can keep faking it to fit in at this crazy company where everyone bows down to his abuse. For several hours after he humiliated me in front of my colleagues, I felt both furious and depressed. I wasn't sure whether to quit and tell him off or just shut down and swallow my feelings one more time."

REGAINING YOUR SENSE OF STRENGTH AND PROFESSIONALISM

The Door Number Three method that helped Krista (and thousands of other men and women who have tried it) is a technique called Quick Refocusing. It can reliably help you regain your clarity and professionalism even when someone at work is criticizing you or disrespecting you. Rather than letting yourself get shut down or defeated, quickly give yourself these silent instructions:

Take a deep breath in and out.

Listen for anything useful or valuable about what could work better next time.

Ignore the disgusting tone of voice, because this person's drama performance is not about you.

Right now is a good time to stay calm and professional, even if this person is incapable of being calm and professional.

Some people memorize these lines and have them ready in case they need a Quick Refocusing on a stressful day. Others carry them on a note card in their wallet or purse to read silently during a private moment to defuse a crisis. Still others rewrite these phrases in their own words.

"MY BOSS LOOKED SURPRISED THAT I WASN'T SHUTTING DOWN"

Krista got a chance to use this powerful technique just a few days after our therapy session. She was in another high-stress meeting with her boss when he started criticizing the way she handled an especially difficult customer. Instead of falling into a sense of defeat or striking back in defense, Krista paused and said to herself, "Take a deep breath in and out. Listen for anything useful or valuable about what could work better next time. Ignore the disgusting tone of voice because this person's drama performance is not about you. Right now is a good time to stay calm and professional, even if this person is incapable of being calm and professional."

According to Krista, "Just saying those words silently to myself changed something about our interaction. Instead of feeling guilty or embarrassed, I felt like a strong adult woman listening to an irate two-year-old."

Krista also said, "My boss looked surprised that I wasn't shutting down or feeling bad about myself this time. He could sense there was something different about the way I was sitting there fully alert, calmly professional, and not at all intimidated by him. He even asked, 'Are you hearing what I'm saying?' and I responded in a calm, strong tone of voice, 'Absolutely, I'm hearing every word you're saying.' My boss did a double-take and for a moment he actually stopped his verbal assault. I guess it's not as satisfying for a bully to keep yelling if the other person isn't quaking."

Skill #2: Know Your Comeback Lines

In addition to breathing smoothly, staying strong with her Quick Refocusing method, and not being intimidated, Krista had also practiced in my office a few powerful comeback lines. You can use them, too, to regain your balance at a moment when some powerful insider at work is being abusive, manipulative, or demeaning.

Especially if there's a part of you that is anxious or uncomfortable about what to say to an arrogant person who breathes down your neck or tries to push you around at work, these lines can boost your sense of self-confidence and professionalism:

- ⌘ *Comeback Line #1 (spoken in a calm, reassuring, and professional tone of voice):* "Time out. What you're saying is important. Let's slow it down and really examine what we can do next time to improve how we handle situations like this."
- ⌘ *Comeback Line #2 (also spoken in a calm, reassuring, and professional tone of voice):* "Okay. I think I understand what isn't working. Now we both need to brainstorm what we can do next time to fix this problem. You go first, and when you're done making some suggestions, I'll offer my own sense of how to improve the situation."

You will notice immediately that both of these comeback lines sound as if you are a strong and competent leader. You don't sound like a passive victim. But neither are you adding fuel to the fire by saying something defensive, sarcastic, or dismissive of the other person's point of view. Rather, you are making sure that everyone in the room perceives you as a trustworthy and sensible individual, a caring and inclusive person who is a key member of the team.

As soon as you calmly say the words "time out" or "okay," and you let the other person go first in offering his or her ideas, you cool him or her down several degrees. Rather than escalating a nasty power struggle, you defuse it for a moment as you gently facilitate a productive brainstorming give-and-take.

I have found in many work settings—profit and nonprofit, traditional and nontraditional—that both of these strong, centered comeback lines can switch you in less than a minute from being the object of this person's anger to being the competent professional who can help lead the team to a realistic solution. You may need to practice these lines a few times with a counselor, coach, or friend before they start to feel natural, so that these words will sound soothing rather than confrontational or disrespectful coming out of your mouth. But if you do decide to use them in a stressful situation at work, I predict that you will be treated much better by the people who formerly viewed you as a doormat or a scorned outsider.

"I COULD SEE HIM CALMING DOWN"

Here's what happened when Krista began using the two comeback lines with her verbally abusive boss. "I'm not a big sports fan," she explains, "but I have seen how the quarterback or the team captain puts his right hand up and covers it like a 'T' with his left palm. So when my boss started scolding me again in front of my colleagues, I decided to try out one of the comeback lines. I put my hands into the shape of a 'T' and said calmly, 'Time out. What you're saying is important. Let's slow it down and really examine what we can do next time to improve how we handle situations like this.'"

Krista said, "It felt great not to be falling back into my old habit of sulking like a resentful victim whenever my boss starts yelling. As soon as I said the words 'Time out, what you're saying is important,' I could see him calming down a little and taking me seriously. I really do believe that when my boss is upset about something at work his emotionality is very much like that of a teething toddler. When I looked at him calmly and said reassuringly, 'Let's slow it down and really examine what we can do,' it was like saying reassuringly to my two-year-old nephew, 'Let's slow it down and find the missing binky. We'll look for it together and we won't stop until we find it.'"

Like many gentle and unconventional people I have counseled, Krista learned quickly, when facing a stressful personality clash at work, how to stop slipping back into self-doubt, thinking "Am I in the wrong field?" or "Maybe I don't have what it takes to make it in this work environment." Instead, she began to experience the feeling of being a strong, competent manager even when she was faced with a screaming boss or a manipulative co-worker. Yes, she was still something of an outsider in the narrow world of this dictator-driven company. But her increased sense of professionalism and her improved leadership skills were earning her new respect from her colleagues and from several of her clients.

For the next few months, Krista successfully used Quick Refocusing and one or both of the Comeback Lines many times to calm her irate boss and others at work. They worked so well that after a few months, she decided to conclude her therapy sessions and to call me only if she wanted to work on a different issue.

Skill #3: Know What to Do If You Are Faced with Something Unethical, Illegal, or Dangerous

Like many of my clients, as they get stronger and clearer emotionally, Krista soon began to outgrow her job. Coming to work month after month and watching her colleagues continue to put up with her boss's temper tantrums, scolding, and ethical lapses began to get old. Ten months after she ended her therapy, Krista called me and said, "I need a follow-up session. I think it's time to start developing an exit strategy."

She explained, "My boss is becoming more sleazy and unethical than ever. There are things I used to ignore but that I now realize could drag me into my own little Enron situation here. I don't need to stay in this job much longer to sense how this corporate soap opera is going to play out."

As soon as I heard Krista say she was thinking about an "exit strategy," I asked her, "How quickly are you planning to give notice?" She laughed and said, "Maybe tomorrow. Maybe next week. I can't imagine staying much longer than that."

A few days later, Krista came in and we began to discuss the fact that there is a fine art to designing an exit strategy without shooting yourself in the foot. Over the past twenty years I've helped hundreds of honest, decent, creative men and women prepare sensible, well-crafted exits from workplace situations that were no longer healthy for them.

⌘ A very creative woman in brand management was tired of making her arrogant and manipulative bosses rich, so she eventually went out on her own. Yet her nine-month exit strategy was so well designed that she was able to generate an enormous amount of new business from her continued rapport with her former co-workers, clients, and suppliers. Every day during those nine months, she spent at least an hour before or after work refining her business plan and deepening her connection to the individuals who later became her best allies, supporters, and leads in her new business.

⌘ A highly unconventional man who designed computer security systems for many years for a stingy, ungrateful boss finally learned in counseling how to develop the people skills and cash-flow strategies to start his own company. For almost eighteen months, this introverted and somewhat socially awkward man slowly improved his negotiation and sales skills, while also expanding his network of financial and technical advisors, until he was ready to go out on his own. He had always thought he was doomed to a life of being up-to-date about computers but clueless about office politics. But once he began to learn—by actually taking some university extension courses—the precise people skills that didn't come naturally to him, he eventually became successful in his own computer security company.

⌘ A very gentle and sensitive woman, a middle-level program manager at a high-stress nonprofit organization, had been unable to get away from an abusive boss (or to qualify for a better-paying job in the nonprofit world) until through therapy she opened up to the fundraising and leadership side of nonprofits. During her ten months of counseling, she also met occasionally with a supportive grant-writing expert and made enough contacts in the nonprofit world to leave her abusive boss and become a co-director of a much better agency in her field of expertise.

THE KEY ELEMENTS OF A SUCCESSFUL ESCAPE

If you or someone you know has been suffering emotionally, financially, and spiritually from working in an unhealthy environment for many years, I strongly recommend that when you leave this toxic situation you do so with wisdom and good sense. If possible, the itinerary of your departure should include:

⌘ At least a few sessions with a counselor, friend, mentor, or consultant, not just to discuss what is wrong with the place where you work, but to clarify what skills you need to improve, what technical information will help you in your new job, and how your unique gifts match what's needed in the marketplace, plus cash flow planning and a network of supportive contacts to get you ready for the next chapter in your work life.

⌘ At least a few lunches, phone calls, or informal meetings with competent people who currently work in the environments where you might want to go next, so that you can explore honestly what are some realistic goals for your move.

⌘ A carefully planned "Countdown to Departure," a weekly schedule of steps to help you make good use of your final months in a soon-to-be-over job while waking up each morning with a strong sense of purpose and focus.

⌘ A financial plan (including multiple income streams from a part-time job or other sources) to make sure you and your loved ones will be all right even if your new venture takes longer than you anticipated to start bringing in sufficient income.

⌘ An honest series of conversations with people you trust to discover what you're best suited for—starting your own organization, finding an existing place to work that is healthier than your previous jobs, or partnering with someone else who balances out your skills and personal challenges.

⌘ Complete written documentation, kept under lock and key, of any unethical, controversial, or questionable things you have witnessed at your current place of business. Be sure to include dates and times, other people who saw or heard what you are describing, and what appropriate actions you considered as well as those you took. If you tried to do the right thing but were thwarted or intimidated by someone, you should note your intentions and what blocked you from taking action. You may want to consult with an attorney or a specialist in your field to find out how to protect yourself against getting dragged into someone else's improprieties.

"I'M GLAD I DIDN'T RUSH INTO SOMETHING FOOLISH"

In Krista's case, rather than quitting her job hastily in a day or a week, she decided to take almost six months to plan and execute her exit strategy, which significantly increased the success of the next phase of her career.

First, she consulted with a lawyer to make sure she documented properly each of the ethical violations her boss was asking of her and managed to say no to him without getting fired.

Second, she began to go to breakfast or dinner at least once a week with colleagues, former clients, and new contacts to learn more about the niche she was hoping to develop into her own start-up company.

Third, she explored the possibility of joining an existing small company that already had a great track record for developing new business while serving its clients ethically and treating its employees well.

At the end of nearly five and a half months of careful research and soul-searching (while still paying her bills on time because she hadn't quit her job impulsively), Krista made up her mind. She decided not to take the risk of going solo in the high-risk financial services field, but rather to join the very reputable small firm she had been courting for the past several months.

As Krista told me a year later when I saw her at a shopping mall near my office, "I'm glad I didn't rush into something foolish. If I'd followed my whim and quit immediately, I would have gotten involved with some other crazy company or I would have started working eighty hours a week trying to get my own firm off the ground with no safety net. But instead, I slowly got to know two of the top people at a company where I am now very happy and well compensated. They have the same core beliefs as I do about how to treat clients and employees with respect and decency. It's so much different now working in a sane environment after all those bizarre incidents trying to be a good mommy to an infantile boss."

Skill #4: Use Multiple Income Streams to Pay the Bills While You Feed Your Soul

As I mentioned briefly above, one of the best ways for a unique individual to break free from an abusive boss or an overly demanding customer is to develop multiple income streams. Some people call it a "day job," because they write, act, design, or work on their own creative projects at night or early in the morning while earning steady income from a less exciting job during daylight hours. Others call it a "balanced life" that combines one heartfelt and passionate pursuit with a much less risky second source of income that pays the bills consistently.

During my years as a counselor, I have seen many examples of how multiple income streams can give an unconventional person the freedom and stability to pursue a highly personal, creative, or entrepreneurial quest. See if any of the following individuals sound like you or someone you know.

THE VISUAL ARTIST

Adrianna, an amazing painter and illustrator, almost gave up her artistic pursuits at the age of thirty-two when she got frustrated that she couldn't make a living from her highly original visions. But then in counseling we talked about "multiple income streams" and "day jobs" until Adrianna came up with an idea that could give her the freedom to keep doing her art.

It took a while for her life to become truly balanced, but for the past several years Adrianna has made a good living from purchasing distressed homes, fixing them up, and reselling them at a profit. This income has allowed her and her partner to remodel their own home and put in an extra room in which Adrianna can design and paint for several hours each morning and evening. Once she stabilized her financial situation, Adrianna discovered she had less anxiousness and more hopefulness in her life, which allowed her to be far more effective at finding supporters and buyers for her exquisite art pieces.

THE UNDERPAID ACTIVIST

Dennis, a teacher and a political activist, had hit a rough patch in his marriage, primarily because his wife had hoped he would be able to earn a larger income to support their three young children. When Dennis came in for counseling, he was skeptical about identifying any way of bringing in new income that wouldn't feel like "selling out."

After we brainstormed for a while, he came up with a great idea that balanced his need for extra income with his values as an activist. During his free time on weekends and for an hour each night after dinner, Dennis designed and set up an information clearinghouse for one of his most cherished political causes. This interactive site was funded and supported by several sources of income—from two grants that Dennis wrote, from the donations of like-minded members of the information clearinghouse, and from a few tasteful advertisements that Dennis was willing to place on his site.

THE CASH-STRAPPED CONGREGATION

Gloria, a member of the clergy, was struggling in her quest to stay afloat financially while leading a small but wonderful congregation. She told me, "I've always wanted to be part of a caring community of interesting people where the group is large enough to create meaningful events but small enough for each person to receive individual attention from the spiritual leadership. Yet the problem has always been covering the costs of such a group and being able to pay my bills each month without the kind of lucrative employment contract that they give you in a large, often impersonal congregation."

During our counseling sessions, Gloria and I explored several possible sources of supplementary income that could work with her values and her busy schedule. Since Gloria had trained for many years to learn deep tissue massage and craniosacral therapy, she decided to work part-time each week helping men and women who had been through traumatic events, from car accidents to childhood incidents of physical abuse with lingering effects.

A year after she came up with the idea of combining her congregational leadership position with a part-time career in body work, Gloria told me, "It's been a perfect mix of two very different modes of helping people. In leading the congregation, I'm usually engaged in a mostly verbal conversation, either as the compassionate listener or in giving inspiring talks. Then during the body-work sessions, mostly with people who are not a part of the congregation, I get to be silent and nurturing in a tactile way. In any given week, I feel as if I'm being of service and doing healing work on several different levels—physically, emotionally, spiritually. And the combined income from my two very different jobs is allowing me to feel financially secure for the first time in my life."

THE RELUCTANCE THAT MAY BLOCK YOU

Even though I have seen hundreds of men and women find ways to support their unconventional and heartfelt quests in life by adding a second income, I have also seen many people reluctant to consider the possibility of multiple income streams at all. They say things like:

- ⌘ "I'm an artist, dammit. Don't ask me to do something else for money, because what I really ought to do is just pursue my art."
- ⌘ "I don't have the energy or the patience to be doing two things. I have to focus on just one thing."
- ⌘ "It's only a matter of time before I hit it big. I can't be bothered with anything that might cause me to lose my focus on my number-one goal."
- ⌘ "It feels like a defeat, like I'm admitting that maybe I don't have what it takes to make it in my first choice, if I let myself add a second source of income."
- ⌘ "I'll feel embarrassed if people from one area of my life see me doing this unflattering day job and think less of me as a result."

Before we go on, I have a confession to make. When I was an undergraduate at Kenyon College in Ohio, studying to become a writer, I spent several days during my junior year talking with a visiting instructor on campus—a brilliant playwright and award-winning author who told me that the key to his success as a risk-taking artist came as a result of his life-long day job working for American Airlines.

The writer's name was Tad Mosel, and he'd written many highly regarded and controversial productions, including the films *Up the Down Staircase*, starring Sandy Dennis, and *Dear Heart*, starring Glenn Ford and Geraldine Page. He also wrote for the New York stage *All the Way Home*, a script based on the James Agee novel *A Death in the Family* that won a Pulitzer Prize and the Drama Critics' Circle Award for Best Play. Tad Mosel later won an Emmy as well for writing an acclaimed historical series for PBS called "The Adams Chronicles."

I was only twenty years old when this famous writer told me, "Make sure you get a solid-paying second job if you want to be free to do what your heart longs to do in your primary career." I thought to myself, "No way! This guy's absolutely wrong. I'm not going to spend my life juggling two careers."

But several years later I discovered the wisdom of what he was saying. I found out that in order to pay the bills (and not let down my family) while writing on topics that truly came from my soul, I needed a second income. Thankfully, my "day jobs" as a psychotherapist and a consultant have given me the freedom to pursue the highly personal writing projects and social activism that otherwise I might have had to abandon. Now I know what Tad Mosel meant when he looked into my eyes and said, "Unless you plan on selling out and doing work that means nothing to your soul, make sure you have a strong second source of income. Only then can you negotiate from strength and be more honest and genuine in your creative pursuits."

THE WOMAN WHO SANG FOR FREE

Almost ten years ago a very talented woman named Jeannette visited my office for her first counseling session and gave me a CD of songs she had performed over the years in small venues in front of crowds who adored her. If you like Joni Mitchell, Shawn Colvin, Mary Chapin Carpenter, or Sara McLachlan, you'd love Jeannette's music.

But like many talented singer-songwriters, Jeannette had gotten shortchanged by a dishonest manager and an early recording contract that gave nearly everything to the record company and very little to the artist. In addition, she had taken several years off from the hectic business to take care of her beautiful young daughter, Olivia, who has severe developmental delays.

What Jeannette wanted from therapy was to sort out how to make a good living from pursuing her music again while coming to terms with the losses and struggles of her life thus far. She knew that her type of music was no longer programmed into the mix by the conglomerate decision-makers on most corporate-owned radio stations and that it was unlikely a major music company would invest in her. But she desperately wanted to get back to writing new songs and performing in front of passionate audiences.

In addition, she told me during her first counseling session, "I've spent too many years like the person in the Joni Mitchell song who 'played real good for free.' It's time I got paid a decent income for being a musician. But whatever you do, don't tell me to go get some boring day job. I've worked for some creepy bosses and a number of mind-numbing jobs. I can't do that anymore."

As we talked, however, I began to sense that Jeannette had a gift not only for performing but also for inspiring others with her voice and her courage. Each of her stories about how she had been a compassionate and persistent mom, classroom teacher's aide, speech therapist, and tutor for her daughter made me wonder if there were any multiple streams of income that could arise from Jeannette being such a gifted teacher. Was there some way for her to coach people who needed to open up their voices and express themselves as powerfully as she could express herself in front of an audience?

Eventually I asked Jeannette, "What if a shy child or an anxious adult came to you and said, 'Can you teach me to speak in public and knock the socks off an audience?' Would you help that shy child and that anxious adult, or would you turn them away?"

Jeannette smiled as she said, "You got me with that one. I wouldn't turn them away. I've always been willing to help anyone who wants to learn how to open up their voice and discover the amazing rush of captivating an audience. If someone came to me for help on how to shine in a public setting, there are definitely things I could teach them."

That was the beginning of a series of brainstorming sessions in which Jeannette designed a successful business as a professional voice coach for a wide range of clients. Over the next few years, she earned the most substantial income of her life from helping anxious executives break free of their boring PowerPoint presentations and become truly powerful speakers. She also helped many shy teens and young adults tackle class presentations, book reports, and job interviews with passion and a clearer voice. In addition, she earned large paychecks as a dialogue coach for a number of feature films and television shows, as well as doing a few voice-overs herself on an animated television series.

The stability and financial freedom she gained from these "day jobs" helped Jeannette to pay for the special services she needed for Olivia, and they also gave her some extra cash flow she used to create an outstanding CD of her songs. She sold a good number of them at her initial "comeback" concerts at various small and medium-sized venues. She sent copies to music company managers and producers, who bought the rights to a few of the songs for their own artists to cover. She also landed a recording contract with a small independent label, which gave her a much better financial arrangement than she'd had years ago with the major label that took advantage of her.

I can't say that Jeannette has ever become as famous as Joni Mitchell, Shawn Colvin, Mary Chapin Carpenter, or Sara McLachlan. But if you could see the joy in her face now as she performs again in front of audiences who love her, you would know she has come to terms with who she is.

Like many other extremely talented—or even slightly talented—people I have counseled, Jeannette has found a balanced way to live that includes both good cash flow and passionate creativity. If you are struggling with either the money part or the creativity part of your career—or if you know someone who is—please don't fall into the trap of thinking you have to pursue one or the other. You may find a way to have both. Start by brainstorming with someone who can help you design your own combination of income sources that balances the need to pay your bills with the need to express what's in your heart and soul.

Chapter Six

Coping with Cliques and Closed-Minded Groups

Life holds many mysteries that have baffled scholars for centuries. Where do the socks end up that disappear from the dryer? Why do car alarms go off most on the mornings when you are hoping to catch up on much-needed sleep?

And why do people in groups tend to exclude perfectly decent men and women who could just as easily be included and welcomed? It's not just the red velvet rope and the bouncer at an exclusive nightclub. You can see examples of cliquishness in any kindergarten where a couple of "cool kids" refuse to share their toys with the newcomer who is "different." You see it in junior high and high school, where some of the popular kids are horrified if one of the less popular kids tries to eat at their exclusive lunchroom table. You see it at college social events, where sarcastic big shots get big laughs by making fun of those who don't have "the right stuff."

You may have witnessed cliquishness and closed-mindedness in the workplace, where the slightly unconventional individual is shunned or left out of social interactions by the keepers of the status quo, or in your neighborhood, where a tight-knit group of gossips keeps a running tab of who's acceptable and who's "questionable."

Or you may have noticed cliquishness cropping up among seniors, in social settings and retirement communities where there often seem to be "established insiders" and "excluded outsiders." I have counseled many active and creative senior citizens who tell me, "If you think high school has some nasty cliques and snobs, wait until you meet some of the folks in the inner circle at any Sun Belt community center. They make it painfully clear who's got clout and who doesn't."

Why Do Cliques Form in the First Place?

There are many theories that attempt to explain this pattern of hurtful exclusionary behavior. If you ask most economists, they will tell you that when you have a large number of people competing over just a few prize outcomes, it creates a brutal selection process. If status, power, attention, love, or money is at all scarce, cliques will form to keep the outsiders from gaining access to the precious and limited commodity.

This "economists' explanation" brings to mind a longtime friend of mine named Paula, a talented artist who often competes for grants and for gallery showings of her work. Since only a few people get selected each year for these grants and gallery events, Paula has found that a snobby clique tends to form among the chosen few who sit on the crucial committees of these arts organizations. "You would think that these well-established artists would have compassion for their fellow creative types," Paula says. "But they can be the most nasty, backbiting, and narrow-minded people you'll ever meet."

On the other hand, if you ask most psychologists about the origin of cliques, they will tell you that it's about defending against your own sense of discomfort by making someone else uncomfortable instead. The vast majority of human beings tend to deflect attention from their own insecurities and vulnerabilities through the group bonding that arises from shunning or saying disparaging things about some other vulnerable individual. Most people in groups get a boost when they can make themselves feel superior to someone else whom the group is excluding or verbally trashing.

Many psychological experiments have shown that normally well-mannered and decent people can act mean, oppressive, and closed-minded when they are first made to feel insecure and then given a group to bond with by putting down other, less favored individuals. It's sad but true that most people from all walks of life are capable of treating an innocent outsider coldly or hurtfully if it means winning the approval and safety of social bonding with the select group in which they want to be included.

Even well-educated and highly intelligent men and women often slip into this pattern of bonding with their peers by putting down less conventional individuals. If you don't believe me, go listen in at any academic department meeting and you will hear publish-or-perish scholars cementing their own standing by saying demeaning things about their rivals and colleagues. One of my friends, an acclaimed scholar and tenured university professor, tells me, "There is often more backbiting, cliquishness, and brutal competition in the ivory towers of academia than there is on Wall Street."

A CHAIN REACTION OF SNOBBERY

I first became curious about this issue when I was growing up in Michigan. I saw that many men and women in my home state who had graduated from the highly selective University of Michigan tended to look down on and say condescending things about the people who had graduated from the less selective Michigan State University, who in turn felt superior to and said condescending things about those who'd attended Eastern Michigan University, who in turn looked down on and said mean things about those who'd gone to Oakland County Community College, who in turn felt superior to and said insulting things about those who hadn't gone to college at all.

Just change the names of the schools to describe the hierarchy of group condescension that you witnessed in your own upbringing. Maybe in your circle of friends the person who went to Princeton looked down on the one who went to Brown, who spoke disparagingly about the one who went to Denison, who made jokes about the one who went to Fairleigh Dickinson, who was rude to the one who got a job right out of high school, and so on. Or maybe your friend who lives in a huge house with a yard sneers at your other friend who lives in a quaint cottage, who in turn looks down on another friend who lives in a tiny apartment.

You must admit it's rather sad that so many human beings on this snobby food chain define their own worth by putting down someone else's life path or personal choices. It makes you wonder if it's possible for human beings to appreciate their own hard-earned wisdom and their own capabilities without framing someone else as a failure or an outcast.

I am reminded of an exquisite spiritual teaching that I didn't fully appreciate when I first heard it as a teenager. Now I think it points to something far more important than SAT scores, how much you can afford to pay for housing, or where your family could afford to send you for an education. This ancient teaching asks, "Who is the person who can truly claim to be a wise individual?"

The answer is, "The one who has true wisdom is the person who listens to and learns from each precious human soul."

RESPONDING BETTER TO HURTFUL CLIQUES

I cannot promise you any 100 percent assured solutions for dealing with snobs or cliquish groups in your own life (or in the life of someone you love). But over the years I've discovered a few sensible strategies that can help you change the way you respond (both internally and externally) in situations where you are outnumbered by people who are rude, unkind, or outright insulting. See which ones you've used already and which ones you may want to try in the future.

Strategy #1: Find Moments of Service to Offset the Moments of Discomfort

Each day of your life, you choose what to focus on and what to ignore. Unfortunately, the human brain is a problem-seeking mechanism. In a group situation, it tends to focus more on the exclusion you experience than on the things that go well. If you spend two hours at a social event and there are ten minutes of painful interactions along with more than a hundred minutes of good interactions, your brain will most likely focus for hours, days, or months on the ten minutes of painful interactions. This is why you dwell on the moments when someone in a group is dismissive toward you or someone you would like to protect, while you barely register or remember the good moments when you did feel connected, included, or involved.

But you can override the problem-obsessed programming of the human brain by deliberately choosing to notice and draw strength from the small successes you attain in each of your group interactions. For example, here is a quick illustration of an interesting person from my counseling practice who made a conscious effort to deal more effectively with cliques by refocusing in a very specific way.

THE SHY WOMAN WHO SAT ALONE

Alissa, a very considerate and somewhat shy woman, had been trying to find a comfortable and inspiring place to attend worship services in her neighborhood. But at each congregation she visited, she found hypocrisy, cliquishness, and phoniness. "People would call themselves spiritual," she told me, "but then you'd see them gossiping or saying mean things behind someone's back."

In addition, Alissa felt self-conscious and isolated at many of these services. She didn't feel comfortable making small talk with the person next to her or trying to make friends at the coffee hours and sweet tables following the services. "Everyone else in the congregation seemed to be conversing with friends or family, and I was usually by myself, sticking out like a sore thumb."

In counseling, we explored Alissa's lifelong discomfort with large groups. She admitted, "It's not just a problem where I go to services. It's been a frustrating issue in my jobs and my social life. I feel as if the world is run by superficial, chatty extroverts who talk a lot but say very little of substance. The much smaller percentage of people who are gentle, quiet, reflective, or bookish tend to fade into the background while these social butterflies suck up all the energy in the room."

During one of our conversations, I asked Alissa, "Even though you're basically a private person, would you be willing to try an experiment that has worked for many people to help them break through and feel connected in large groups?"

Alissa replied, "That depends on what the experiment requires me to do."

So I explained, "The experiment I've seen work effectively is to find a pleasurable way of volunteering each week in order to be of service to someone in the congregation. Since you've got a great heart and a warm smile, you could sign up to be a greeter each week before and after services to help the new arrivals feel welcome. Or you could volunteer to be part of the child-care team, the set-up team, the clean-up team, the retreat weekend planning committee, or the group that calls and visits those who are ailing. Or you could be a part of the weekly study group. Instead of letting your brain focus on the cliques in the congregation, you could consciously find a way to make genuine contact, one person at a time, with the non-snobs who probably have been feeling as isolated as you."

Alissa was skeptical. "I've tried it before in other congregations," she claimed, "and it doesn't really work to sign up for some committee. Especially since the heads of the volunteer committees tend to be the superficial extroverts who say they care deeply about you but it's clear they don't. There is so much phoniness to contend with."

I replied, "I agree with what you've been saying about the cliques in many congregations. But I hope you'll try this experiment for just three months, because that seems to be the minimum amount of time it usually takes to make noticeable progress in a cliquish situation. If you see it as a personal experiment and you let yourself make a serious commitment to volunteer at something you might enjoy, where you are a part of an imperfect human team for at least three months, let's be scientific about it and see what happens."

Since it was a relatively short commitment, Alissa decided to give it a try. First she signed up to be a greeter for newcomers at the weekly services; eventually she began to attend an intensive study group that met weekly to explore in depth a passage of a sacred text or an issue in spiritual life.

However, during her first couple of weeks as a volunteer, Alissa's frustrations got worse. As she described it, "There are some real ego problems in this congregation. Especially the big donors who have clout because of how much they contribute financially, but act in ways that are completely in opposition to the teachings and practices that we're exploring in the study group."

But after two months of volunteering as part of the greeter team and going deeper into the study session topics each week, something began to shift in Alissa's perception of the congregation. "It's strange," she told me. "The phoniness is definitely still there among many of the big shots who've been committee chairs for many years. Yet there are a few good people I've come to know and respect. I happened to say hello to each of them spontaneously while I was doing my greeter job every week and trying to make people feel welcome and included. In fact, there's one woman I was friendly to when she first came to services two months ago who's now in the study group. She's truly a kind soul, and we've been talking privately for a few minutes each week after the formal discussions are over. We've had great conversations, not only about the study topics but also about our real-life dilemmas, and I've recently been invited to meet her and two of her neighbors for a relaxing dinner. There's also one interesting man in the congregation who has impressed me with his thoughtfulness and his involvement in several good causes. He and I have had some long conversations that make me feel as though I'm not really so alone here anymore."

As Alissa discovered, the goal in dealing with a cliquish organization is not to stage a violent coup or insist that all the hypocrites miraculously change overnight. Rather, by being of service and volunteering to be part of a small, inclusive team for at least three months, Alissa—like several of my other clients—found that even a perennial outsider can feel welcomed and at home in a large group. It's as Mahatma Gandhi said: we each need to be the change we want to see. By focusing your attention on ways to be of service and create one-on-one moments of genuine connection, you may turn the group that used to intimidate you into a setting where you can shine in your own heartfelt way.

I urge you to try this experiment in your own life. Whether it's a congregation where you have felt isolated or some other setting—a nonprofit organization, a neighborhood committee, a parent-teacher association—all it takes is one meaningful volunteer moment of profound connection, or one positive ally, to change the way you feel about the group. You might still be a shy person, and I'm not asking you to become a chatty phony. But when you find, in the midst of a large group, that there are at least a few gentle souls who don't put on airs, the imperfections of the overall situation will fade into the background. You will have begun the process of identifying a subgroup, the like-minded friends who understand and appreciate your way of being. (For more specific tools on how to develop trustworthy allies and supporters even when the majority of a group doesn't share your beliefs or values, please see Chapters Eight, Nine, and Ten.)

Strategy #2: Recognize that Many Excluders Are Secretly Doing a Cover-Up

At first glance the fashionably dressed, outgoing men and women you observe from afar at dinner parties, religious services, neighborhood gatherings, or your workplace may seem intimidating. They often look as if they've got it all together—that their lives are a lot smoother and more successful than yours or mine.

But I can assure you that looks are deceiving. As a therapist, I have spent thousands of hours listening to people who look great on the outside and have impressive resumes, but are troubled on deeper levels they rarely show in public. In fact, those who spend the most time and energy trying to look flawless and intimidating often have the greatest secret fears of one day "losing it all" or being "found out." Ironically, the person who has the most painful buried secrets is often the one in the group who acts most like a sarcastic know-it-all or serves as the status gatekeeper deciding who's in and who's out.

That's why I strongly urge you, the next time you are dealing with a cliquish group, to ask yourself these helpful questions:

✂ Is there someone in this group who acts like a powerful insider, but who I know (or sense) is hiding a secret vulnerability or a history of insecure feelings underneath all that bravado?

⌘ Is there some way I can stop putting these secretly insecure people higher than they deserve to be?

⌘ Am I feeling intimidated by someone in the group who's actually hiding his or her vulnerabilities, or am I trying too hard to please these hard-to-please people, which is turning me into a false self I don't want to be?

No matter how intelligent or perceptive you are, it's quite possible that you have been fooled by at least one insecure person who's intimidated you by looking so picture-perfect. For example, have you ever experienced anything like the situation described in the next few paragraphs?

THE SIX-FOOT-FOUR-INCH INTIMIDATING EXPERT

Several years ago I was trying to break into a cliquish situation in order to get accepted as a part-time instructor at a very prestigious educational institution. I will disguise a few details to protect the guilty. But let me just say that this incident helped me appreciate the pain and frustration of feeling shut out by an intimidating individual in a group that operates on the principle of exclusion.

In applying to be one of the few instructors in this program, I had made many phone calls, sent several carefully composed e-mails, gone on three interviews, provided letters of endorsement, and done everything I could to get accepted. But there was one particular insider who didn't want me to get in. He is a brilliant, articulate, scholarly, and noticeably tall (a six-foot-four-inch) expert in his field who seems to enjoy ripping apart his opponent in any debate.

I'll be honest with you—I did feel intimidated by this guy. Each time I met him in person, I felt as if he had a much better education than I did and his clout in important circles was much greater than mine would ever be.

During one of our face-to-face conversations, he told me point-blank that therapists are a menace to society and that they don't belong in the world of academia because the field of psychology is so imprecise and unscientific. Then he turned his anger on someone else in the room. After chewing this person up and spitting him out, he looked at me and said,

"There is nothing better than the feeling of eviscerating some rival's point of view." He actually used that word; he liked to rip the guts out of someone.

The delight on his face as he said "eviscerate" reminded me of Robert Duvall's character in *Apocalypse Now* who says, "I love the smell of napalm in the morning," while the Vietnamese families run screaming and the huts go up in flames. I felt awkward and clumsy around this guy, as if I was trying too hard to win his approval or avoid his wrath.

Then, a few days before the final selection was to be made, my wife and I went to the movies at Century City Shopping Center in West L. A. Before our movie started, I went to the large public restroom. There I overheard a man in one of the stalls screaming at his five-year-old son, who was having trouble urinating accurately into the toilet. The man was getting more and more impatient, which just made the little boy even more upset and out of control.

Suddenly I saw out of the corner of my eye that the man now exiting the stall, the grown man who was so agitated by his young son, was this very same six-foot-four-inch intimidating expert. He didn't see me. But all of a sudden I didn't feel intimidated by this arrogant and abrasive individual anymore.

After I washed my hands and left the restroom, I said a silent prayer of thanks that a compassionate God, or possibly the mysterious connectivity of the universe, had let me have this important piece of information about someone in whose presence I'd formerly felt insecure. When I got back to the movie theater, I said to my wife, "I just saw one of the saddest things in the world. I saw a very intelligent man who had no clue how to be caring and patient toward the son I'm sure he loves."

WHO'S AFRAID OF WHOM?

What I saw at the Century City Shopping Center bears out what I've found many other times in my life: the cliquish men and women who act the most arrogant, intimidating, and abrasive are often the most terrified or fragile on some hidden level. It's like when you go hiking in the desert and come up against a hissing snake. The snake may seem scary to you, but in fact the snake is hissing in great fear; it sees you as a huge threat, especially since you tower over its narrow, earthbound body. Or if you are camping in the woods and you hear about a ferocious bear that has been spotted in the vicinity, the odds are the bear is terrified because someone has gotten dangerously close to its cubs.

The same holds true in most cliquish groups. For some reason, you and I (the outsiders) are a frightening threat to the power, control, or status quo of the insiders. They are often more afraid of us—and the changes we might bring to the group—than we are of them.

A few months after I heard the six-foot-four-inch intimidating expert yelling at his son in the public restroom, I found out from a mutual friend why this powerful insider resented me so much and wanted to block my appointment to be on the staff of his institution. This large but secretly vulnerable man not only had problems with his five-year-old son; he had also been estranged for many years from his controlling eighty-year-old father. My friend told me that this brilliant, aggressive scholar was threatened by the notion of having me on staff because I had written two books on how to reconcile with parents and other complicated relatives. Since this was a painful and upsetting subject for him, he didn't want me around.

When I heard the reason why I was being excluded, I felt both a twinge of frustration and a twinge of compassion. It was frustrating to have a powerful insider make things difficult and put my goal out of my reach because of his own unresolved issues. But I also felt for this fragile and wounded soul in a six-foot-four-inch frame struggling with so much unresolved family distress. I realized that his anxiety about psychotherapy, his awkwardness with his son, and his estrangement from his father were far more severe than the distress I had been going through while waiting for a decision about a part-time teaching job.

MAKING THE CRUCIAL SWITCH FROM INTIMIDATION TO COMPASSION

What about in your own life or in the life of someone you know? Have you felt intimidated or sensed you were trying too hard to please someone who was being evasive, rude, dismissive, or insensitive? Have you ever doubted your own self-worth because a particular group didn't let you in?

If you are very lucky, then God or the universe may give you a peek into the deeper layers of pain and fear that are causing this person or this group to shun you. You might discover that the rejection has very little to do with you or your worth and a lot more to do with the insecurities and fears of change that are churning inside the others.

But in many cases, you won't see or hear a specific clue as to why you are being left out or treated coldly. At those moments you will need at least one strong ally or friend who can say to you honestly, "Don't give up who you are and what your life is about just because this particular group isn't letting you in. You're worth a lot more than you realize." (For more specific tools and strategies on how to stay strong and be effective even when a particular group isn't ready yet for the changes and ideas you are offering them, please see Chapter Eight.)

Strategy #3: Always Be on the Lookout for Members of the Inner Circle Who Are Flexible Enough to Make a Side Deal with You

When you are an outsider looking in, the members of a cliquish group seem at first glance to be unified, undivided, and in full agreement about everything. There are few visible signs of dissent, diversity, or flexibility as you watch a powerful group of insiders doing their thing.

But once again, you must remember that looks are deceiving. In my experience, even cliquish groups that appear to be inflexible usually have one or two individuals who are open to new ideas, diverse viewpoints, or building bridges with someone who is on the outskirts of the group. It may take a while to identify and develop a rapport with these embedded rebels and free thinkers in disguise. Yet if you want to be successful in dealing with any cliques where you live, where you work, or where you have personal involvements, you will need to learn the best ways to connect and maintain the trust of these individuals who may be willing to stray from the rigid confines of the cliquish group.

THE WOMAN WHO WAS A PARIAH IN HER OWN BUILDING

Here's an illustration of what I mean by identifying a possible bridge-builder. One of my clients, a wonderful special-education teacher and divorced mom named Geena, moved into a very nice condominium complex a few years ago that had some great amenities, including a pool, an exercise room, a comfortable meeting room with sofas and chairs, and a good security system. Geena was excited about starting a new chapter of her life in this well-planned community and immediately applied to take part in the monthly meetings of the condo board. That's when her problems began.

According to Geena, "Trying to get your good ideas taken seriously by this condo board is about as easy as being a vegan at the beef marketers' annual convention. From the moment I walked into the first board meeting and mentioned that I sometimes have special-education kids over for a get-together with my ten-year-old son, you could see the horror in the eyes of the most powerful insiders. In addition, I was the only unmarried woman at the meetings, where the older married men and their possessive wives looked at me as if I was wearing a T-shirt that said 'Homewreckers.com.' It felt very creepy to be viewed as a threat in the very place I was hoping would finally feel like 'home.' I even heard one woman whisper a bit too loudly to her husband, 'I didn't know we were letting in people with kids.'"

For the first twenty months that Geena lived in this building, she felt isolated and uncomfortable when she ran into other residents at the pool, in the exercise room, in the elevator, in the garage, or in the hallways. At first she tried to ignore the cold looks and the suspicious eyes that followed her as she walked with her son past couples who seemed much more affluent and more conservative than she. Then she decided to try to make some suggestions at the monthly board meetings about opening up the application process so that other moms with young kids might get accepted into the community.

When she first came in for therapy to discuss the stress she was feeling from her teaching job, her difficulties in being a single mom, and her struggles to find suitable partners through online dating, Geena hadn't planned to tell me about the sense of tension and estrangement she was experiencing where she lived. But as soon as I asked her, "What's the biggest contributor to the sense of frustration you live with on a daily basis?" her eyes filled with tears. She told me, "I have always been someone who can get along with most people. But right now where I'm living I'm treated like a pariah and I don't know how to make it better."

That was when we began to explore the strategy of identifying secret rebels, possible exceptions to the monolithic compliance of the condo clique. I asked Geena, "Have there been any moments yet when someone broke out of cold-shoulder mode and showed you or your son just a little bit of kindness or caring?"

Geena thought for a moment. "There's one woman on the board who has a granddaughter the same age as my son. A few weeks ago the grand-daughter was visiting her for the weekend and my son played well with her in the swimming pool for a few minutes. But then as soon as some of the powerful board members showed up at the pool, the woman took her granddaughter and left. I wasn't sure if she really had some appointment she needed to go to, or whether she also senses it's not comfortable having kids at this place."

TAKING THE RISK OF REACHING OUT

For the rest of that counseling session, we explored ways to talk with the grandmother of the girl who was the same age as Geena's son. We discussed which words and phrases might feel too invasive, too needy, too desperate, or too rebellious, in case the grandmother wasn't willing yet to be honest about what it's like for her to bring her granddaughter to a place that doesn't appreciate young children. Finally, we came up with a few nonthreatening ways of opening up a conversation with this grandmother to find out if she shared any of the same feelings of isolation or discomfort that Geena had been feeling.

A few days later, Geena ran into the woman at the mailbox and struck up a conversation. She asked, "How's your granddaughter?" and gently mentioned that she'd been impressed at how mature the granddaughter was, how patient and generous with her pool toys when Geena's son asked if they could trade.

Geena recalled, "The grandmother looked around as if she were living in East Germany at the time of the Stasi secret police. When she saw there was no one else who could hear her, she whispered to me, 'My grand-daughter really enjoyed playing with your son. She often feels frustrated because there are no other kids to play with when she comes here to visit me. She told me on the phone yesterday that she wants to come back and visit when that nice boy is at the pool again.'"

Geena saw one of the board members approaching the mailbox, so she didn't pursue it any further. But a few days later she had a long conversation with the nice grandmother about how lonely and awkward it had been for both of them to be dealing with a powerful clique of condo board members who apparently didn't want kids around.

As with many of my clients who have been up against rigid and unwelcoming cliques, it only took one other secret rebel to change the way Geena felt about where she lived. Over the next six months, Geena and the grandmother became good friends and arranged several successful play dates for the two children. "It feels so different now to just know I'm not completely alone," Geena says. "Yes, there is still a bizarre cult of kid-haters running the board meetings. But I've spoken privately with an open-minded person from the management company, and he's assured me that he's going to let in a few more families with school-age children in spite of what the condo board has been saying. It may take years to make significant changes in how the long-time residents treat kids who come to visit the pool or how they view divorced moms like me. But at least this one stressful area of my life has gotten a little easier."

HOW TO SPOT A POTENTIAL BRIDGE-BUILDER

It could have happened differently for Geena. Even with the right words and phrases, she might have approached the grandmother and found her unable to break ranks with the cliquish insiders on the condo board. But if you find the right moment to open up the conversation, you might locate a bridge-builder. You might identify someone who has been feeling just as mistreated by the clique as you have.

Think about the closed-minded groups you currently have to deal with at work, in volunteer organizations, in your neighborhood, or in your social circles, and ask yourself these questions:

⌘ Is there at least one person who has the potential to share my point of view or know my concerns because he or she has had a similar painful experience?

⌘ Is there at least one person who has shown a moment of kindness or caring in contrast to the coldness of the other group members?

⌘ Is there someone among the powerful insiders who seems to have enough self-esteem, independence, or rebelliousness to occasionally break the code of compliance that is keeping the other insiders from listening to any new viewpoints?

⌘ Is there a particular time or setting where one or more group members tend to let down their defenses a bit, where they might be willing to brainstorm with you about how to make some positive changes?

Once again, I'm not promising any overnight miracles. You might find it takes months or even years before a crack in the rigid code of compliance reveals itself. But just as the Colorado River slowly carved an opening through the huge ancient rocks to create the Grand Canyon, nature tells us that rigid structures eventually give way to water, which seems less powerful but never stops flowing. Even if the cliquish groups in your life look as immovable as ancient rock, put your money on the flowing river, because sooner or later the water always creates an opening.

Chapter Seven

Finding Peace with Your Family

A few years ago I was on a national media tour for my book *When Difficult Relatives Happen to Good People.* At a television station in a major city, I was scheduled to be interviewed by the very well-liked host of a popular talk show. A few minutes before the show was to start, the host, an elegantly dressed woman with perfect makeup and impeccable hair, walked quickly onto the set where I was seated by myself.

She leaned close to me and said in a low voice, "Dr. Felder, I don't want to talk about this during the interview. But I do want to hear from you off-camera what I should do about my family situation. My parents and my two older siblings still treat me horribly. Every year at family get-togethers, I go through the motions and try to pretend nothing is wrong. I've always been the outcast in my family—the only one with liberal views and the only one who isn't married and who doesn't have two-point-eight kids. No matter how much I accomplish in life, they still treat me like I'm a disappointment in their eyes. What can I do to improve the way I'm treated by my own flesh and blood?"

For a moment, there was genuine sadness in her eyes. Then she quickly put on her lapel microphone and got back into character as the award-winning TV journalist everyone expected her to be. But I was struck once again by this glimpse of a widespread reality: no matter how much we accomplish as adults, we still often feel estranged from certain family members who judge us harshly.

When the on-camera interview was done, I stayed around until the entire program was over and then spoke with the host for almost an hour. Like many other intelligent men and women who seem on the surface to be competent and functioning well, she was secretly torn apart inside from the coldness and criticism she received from her closest relatives. I remember vividly the look on her face as she asked me, "Will it ever get better? Will I ever be able to spend time with my own family and not feel so painfully alone?"

When Did It Start for You?

After years of researching this topic, I can safely say that in our society, there are tens of millions of men and women like this talk-show host—good and decent individuals who carry deep invisible scars from feeling isolated while growing up in families that refused to accept their differences or recognize that being different might be a positive attribute. This lonely feeling that you're a fish out of water in your own family can be a recurring problem that tugs at your shaky sense of well-being year after year. No matter how far you move away from your relatives or how infrequently you see them face-to-face, you may still worry, "Maybe there's something wrong with who I am."

If you feel emotionally distant from judgmental or harsh relatives—or if someone you love does—when exactly did it begin? When did you first realize that you were being treated like an outsider in your own family?

As you look at the six possibilities below, note which of these describe most accurately the moments in your own life when you were viewed as a troublemaker, a "disappointment," or a fifth wheel in your family of origin:

✂ *Did it happen between age 17 and 25?* Many people feel close to their families through childhood and up to early adulthood, when they may pick a career, a lifestyle, or a divergent path that goes against the family's hopes. Suddenly you've fallen out of favor because you're not meeting the expectations others had for you.

- *Did it happen because of your sexual or romantic life?* Some people feel connected to their families until they fall in love with someone whom their relatives don't accept. Or the rough times begin when you marry into a family that is unwelcoming or disapproving of you. Every year at family gatherings you can feel the tension when relatives look at you (and your beloved) with eyes that seem skeptical or hostile.
- *Did it happen when you started speaking up?* Some people feel accepted by their families until they start to discover their own opinions and values. Then when they start speaking up to change what isn't healthy about their families, others are shocked and horrified. Quite often a family would rather ostracize the member who challenges the status quo than stop and hear the legitimate concerns he or she is trying to express.
- *Did a rift happen after a painful loss or tragedy?* Some people feel close to their families until a divorce, a separation, a death, an addiction, or some other major shake-up splits the family into factions. Even if no one will admit there's an elephant in the room, any reasonable person can see that this family is being torn apart by something that they are unwilling to discuss or resolve.
- *Did it happen as soon as you started to reveal that you were different in a family that prizes conformity?* If you were hyperactive, shy, creative, rebellious, imaginative, or original, your family may have begun to turn away from you because they were too busy (or too shallow) to deal with your legitimate questions and concerns. Even at a very young age, you may have felt your family's disapproval or disappointment because, instead of someone compliant or predictable, they got someone "interesting" and "challenging."
- *Did it happen even before you were old enough to speak?* Some people never felt particularly loved or welcomed by their families because there were certain individuals who never accepted their presence (perhaps because the new arrival took away their own special place in the family). Rather than being welcomed into your family with open

arms, you may have felt isolated or underappreciated from the beginning because of such competitive tensions or family struggles.

What Can Be Done to Improve a Frustrating Family Situation?

If one or more of these possibilities stirs up painful memories for you, I strongly urge you to talk with a supportive counselor or friend to sort out the truth about your upbringing. It's extremely important to make sure the long-standing family stressors in your life don't hold you back from having the career satisfaction, relationship success, and positive sense of self-worth that you deserve to have. Even though you might not be able to change the core personality of certain family members, you *can* change the way you respond to them and determine whether or not your family issues will continue to drain your energy year after year.

That's why the rest of this chapter will focus primarily not on rehashing the personality clashes of the past, but on crafting creative options for the present and future. From this day forward, what will improve your way of dealing with your extended family in its current form? What will give you a stronger sense of inclusion and respect each year at holiday gatherings and other emotionally charged family events? What will help you move beyond the frustrations from your earlier struggles with your family so that you can try something new and more effective with them?

Creative Option #1: Take a Few Moments to Immunize Yourself Against Your Family's Most Frustrating Words

I've found that in nearly every family situation where someone feels judged or outnumbered, there are specific words and phrases the family uses repeatedly to inflict shame, guilt, or coercive control on its most independent-thinking members. If you want to deal more effectively with the tensions in your own family, it's crucial to figure out what these emotionally loaded words are and to immunize yourself for the next time your family tries to control you with them.

For example, when someone in your family is trying to win an argument or get you to do things his or her way, does he or she employ any of the following "Most Likely to Cause Guilt or Shame" comments?

- ⌘ "You're too sensitive."
- ⌘ "You're selfish."
- ⌘ "Don't upset your father (or mother)."

If you hear these phrases whenever there is a power struggle in your family, especially from people who are so deeply connected to you on a soul level, it often makes you feel unsure of yourself. You might think, "Are they right? Am I really too sensitive? Maybe I *am* being selfish. Or maybe it's not good to be upsetting my father, even if he is being a creep right now."

When you get bombarded with shame-inducing comments like the three classics listed above, you might notice that you begin to feel grumpy, sad, depressed, powerless, thwarted, or shut down. Or you might start craving a stiff drink or massive quantities of comfort food.

But if you carefully take apart and honestly examine the true intention behind each of these guilt-inducing comments, you may learn to have a different and more effective response the next time your family tries to use one of them on you. If you want to understand the deeper meaning and sneaky purpose of these phrases, consider the following:

- ⌘ When they say **"you're too sensitive,"** it probably means, "We don't want to apologize or take any responsibility for the fact that we hurt you (or someone you care about whom we don't accept). We'd rather accuse you of being 'too sensitive,' which usually makes you feel insecure and become a bit more compliant. If we make you squirm by calling you 'too sensitive,' we never have to look at our own bad behavior.
- ⌘ When they say **"you're selfish,"** it usually means, "You didn't immediately comply with what we think is the one and only way. Since we aren't willing to be flexible or understanding of what you need, we'd

rather try to shut you down and bully you by calling you 'selfish.' Especially since we know from past experience that when we accuse you of being selfish, you tend to feel guilty and do what we want you to do."

- When they say **"don't upset your father (or mother),"** it often means, "We don't have the patience or the compassion to appreciate what you need in this situation or to work toward a healthy compromise. So we'd rather try to make you feel guilty and get you to do things our way by grabbing hold of your guts and twisting them.'"

THE IMMUNIZATION METHOD IN ACTION

If you know ahead of time that certain members of your family are going to use these or similar shame-inducing lines on you, you can build up your immunity before the next visit or phone call. With a friend, a counselor, a tape recorder, or a private journal, simply repeat the guilt phrases several times. Then say to yourself:

> *I know I'm going to hear my family's favorite traditional guilt-inducing lines.*
> *I'm going to remember to breathe, stay centered, and feel strong and healthy even when they say them again this time.*
> *I'm going to smile deep inside and be grateful that I was able to predict ahead of time, with amazing accuracy, the precise lines that used to shut me down. This time they won't have that same impact on me.*

"DAD, THIS ISN'T THE RIGHT TIME"

One of my counseling clients who successfully used this "Immunization Method" was Monty, a creative and compassionate man in his fourties who grew up with two extremely controlling parents and one bossy older sibling. In Monty's extended family, there is a long tradition of certain family members having a few too many drinks at family gatherings and becoming very negative and critical.

According to Monty, "When my mom, my dad, my uncle, or my older brother has had a bit too much to drink, the unsolicited advice and the sarcastic put-downs start to fly. The more drinks they've had, the more personal and pointed the comments become."

Monty recalls, "A few weeks ago at a family birthday dinner, after several rounds of cocktails my dad started giving me the third degree about my personal finances and the struggles I've had on a few of my creative projects. I tried to get him to stop, especially since I'd brought a new partner to meet my family at this dinner. When my dad wouldn't stop the aggressive questions and demeaning comments, I made one more effort to say calmly and gently, 'Dad, this isn't the right time for us to be having this discussion.'"

As soon as Monty said that to his father, Monty's older brother snapped at him, "Let's face it, Monty. You're just too sensitive."

A few moments later, Monty's mom pulled Monty aside and said, "Don't upset your father. Can't you see he hasn't been feeling well lately? Now look how you're talking to him."

At his next two counseling sessions, Monty and I translated what these lines—"you're too sensitive" and "don't upset your father"—truly mean in Monty's family. According to Monty, "They are the lines that always used to shut me down and get me to go along with the family's way of doing things. What they essentially mean is that Dad is unwilling to control his liquor intake and unable to be civil once he's had too much to drink. Yet the rest of the family always takes his side even when he's being hurtful and obnoxious."

When I asked Monty to tell me more about what the phrase "too sensitive" might mean to him personally, he thought for a moment. Then he said, "It's supposed to mean I'm a wuss. They're trying to imply there's something wrong or shameful about my being 'sensitive.' But if I had to choose between being 'strongly sensitive' or being 'strongly insensitive,' I'd rather be 'strongly sensitive.' When I was very young I hated being called sensitive, yet over the years I've found it actually describes a strength that I don't want to diminish. Being a sensitive person does not make me a wuss—whatever that might be. In fact, it has made me a lot more empathic and tuned into people's feelings than my family ever was."

During our conversations, Monty realized something else. "The line my mom usually hits me with—'don't upset your dad'—essentially means that she's willing to take his side even when he's being hurtful and inappropriate. For years she's been afraid of him, which makes her unable to speak up and ask for what she needs in their one-sided marriage. So when she says 'don't upset your dad,' she's telling me to become the same kind of doormat she's had to be in order to stay married to him. I feel sorry for each of them, but the truth is I don't need to let my father walk all over me just because that's the way things are traditionally done in my family."

In addition to taking these classic phrases apart and seeing what they mean on a deeper level, Monty and I also practiced saying the words "you're too sensitive" and "don't hurt your father" dozens of times in various tones of voice until they lost their painful sting. By saying the words exactly the way they would be said by his mom, his older brother, and his uncle, Monty reclaimed his sense of humor and his sense of inner strength. The phrases no longer had the power to twist his intestines into a knot; now they sounded like empty, sneaky words that could no longer manipulate him or shut him down.

At the next family gathering, it took less than half an hour for Monty to hear his family members saying "you're too sensitive" and "don't upset your father." He told me afterward, "It was a breakthrough for me in how I respond to my family. They tried to use the same guilt trips as before, only this time I was smiling inside and saying to myself, 'Wow, this is fun.' I predicted not only the exact words but the precise tone of voice that they'd use when they were trying to get me to go along with their unhealthy ways of being. I know how the game is played in this family and I don't have to get all guilt-ridden this time."

Creative Option #2: Redefining Your Role

In most families, who gets respect and who doesn't is rigidly defined. Maybe it's the eldest or the richest who gets preferential treatment in your family. Or the one who is most compliant with the wishes of others or loyal to the values of the older generation. Or the one who most closely conforms to the way of being that your family considers the only proper way.

If you're not the eldest, richest, most compliant, or most conforming family member, then you get assigned a different role. You might be the outcast, the rebel, the irritant, the ignored one, or the one who gets blamed for everything that goes wrong.

There comes a time when you begin to outgrow the uncomfortable role your family has assigned to you and you're ready for a healthier way of relating to them. But please don't wait for your family members to call you up on the phone and say, "Hi, we no longer need to keep you locked into that unpleasant role you've been in for so many years." If you're waiting passively for your parents or siblings to call and declare, "We're ready to treat you like a respected equal," all I can say is, "You should live so long." The most important change has to occur first within *you*. That's why it's best to define for yourself a positive and honored identity that you can keep in mind each time you are visiting or talking on the phone with your most difficult family members.

Here are a few possible personas or identities that might help you regain your sense of strength and self-respect even when you're bombarded by negative comments from your relatives. See which of these appeals to you most:

THE WISE AND CALM OBSERVER, TAKING NOTES FOR A BETTER FUTURE

One of the most pleasurable roles that you can take in a difficult family situation is to imagine yourself to be an anthropologist, a journalist, or a family researcher visiting a colorful group of people who are going to provide you with excellent material for an award-winning study.

Simply watch and take note of the fascinating habits, rules, power hierarchies, guilt trips, and other communication patterns that go on in this family. Imagine that you are safely protected by lots of grant money and a guarantee that your research results will be published, so you can pull back and observe at your leisure the intricacies of this unusual and intense configuration of human beings.

I once had a counseling client named Eugenia whose family gatherings used to give her a stomachache and a pounding headache. After we discussed this exercise in therapy, she began taking on the role of the Wise and Calm Observer, in which she imagined she was an anthropologist from a foreign university who had received a substantial grant to observe and make sense of a very contentious or unpleasant family. Eugenia told me afterward, "For the first time ever, I was able to relax my stomach muscles and not get a headache even when my parents, my siblings, and the other relatives were doing some obnoxious and hurtful things. I just watched them calmly with the confidence and relaxed professionalism of an acclaimed anthropologist. Let me tell you—these family interactions were off-the-charts ugly, yet I felt safe and protected from their nonsense."

THE MUCH-NEEDED VOICE OF SANITY

Rather than feeling guilty, ashamed, or frustrated to be seeing things differently from the rest of your family, this second persona lets you honor and embrace differing points of view. You don't have to out-shout your relatives or stoop to their level. You can simply use your most sincere, soothing voice, just as you would if you were a camp counselor calmly supervising a group of impulsive seven-year-olds. The contrast between the unpleasant way people usually address each other in your family and the relaxed, strong voice that you are using will most likely get everyone's attention.

Your soothing Voice of Sanity shouldn't be condescending or patronizing. Rather, you can simply take charge in the middle of a stressful moment and say calmly, "Let's slow down and see what we can do here to make sure everyone gets heard and treated fairly. How about if each person gets two minutes to say their point of view and then we'll come up with a workable solution we can all live with."

I've seen this persona work even for people who did not previously have much clout or influence in their family. One example is my client Lena, who grew up in a traditional family situation where her older brothers and her dad usually got their way and the women were supposed to be good-looking and compliant. During her teenage years, Lena rebelled against the family norms. She often became visibly angry and spoke out whenever a disagreement or an unfair situation occurred in her family. This only made matters worse, because her brothers and her dad tended to roll their eyes and call her the "B word" whenever Lena protested passionately against their domination.

Then in counseling, when Lena was in her twenties, we worked for several weeks on developing a calm, strong Voice of Sanity persona for her. She practiced it several times during our counseling sessions and she began to use it at work when giving helpful feedback to her colleagues or responding to customers who spoke to her aggressively.

A few months later, Lena was at a family weekend gathering where she once again saw her dad and her older brothers dominating a decision about the schedule, which they were arranging to suit only their needs, while ignoring what Lena, her mom, and her two aunts wanted to do. Using her strong, calm, nonthreatening Voice of Sanity, Lena said to her relatives, "Okay, everybody, let's try something new this year. Let's go around the room and each person can suggest one activity that you want to make sure gets included at some point. Then let's work together to devise a schedule that includes either 100 percent of the ideas or as close to 100 percent as we can get. Dad, you go first."

Lena told me, "For a few seconds it was so quiet you could hear a pin drop. In my family, there's never been this kind of respectful, inclusive style of leadership. It's always been dominate or be dominated. So when I asked my dad to go first and I laid out the ground rules, they were in shock for a while. I could see one of my brothers looking at me suspiciously, as if to say, 'What kind of drug has she been taking?' But for the first time in the long history of this family we did make a much better weekend plan that was far more inclusive of each person's needs and preferences than we've ever done before."

THE STUDENT OF HEALTHY HUMAN RELATIONSHIPS, LEARNING WHAT YOU DON'T WANT TO EMULATE

Not every family responds as well as Lena's family did. Sometimes you may use your most calm, soothing Voice of Sanity and the relatives will still explode in arguments, insults, and stubbornness.

This third and final persona is quite effective for helping good people stay strong and relaxed even when they're around very difficult family members. In this third persona, you imagine yourself to be an adult student learning carefully what habits, behaviors, and character traits you *don't* want to repeat in your own life and relationships. It's like you're taking an advanced course in the family legacies and habits you don't want to pass along to the next generations.

It's easy for most people to come up with a list of the traits that they see in their most difficult relatives and don't want to repeat on their own spouses, kids, friends, or guests. Every family gathering is the chance for a vivid illustration of obnoxious behaviors not to emulate.

Monty, whose father and other family members drink too much and become hypercritical, decided to use this student persona to view his family's obnoxious behaviors as a "wonderful teaching moment where I could clarify what specific traits I don't want to permit myself to engage in no matter what."

In my office a few days after an especially unpleasant holiday gathering, Monty made a list of the family behaviors he found hurtful and he raised his right hand to "solemnly swear" he would do everything in his power to make sure he didn't repeat these actions with his own loved ones. On his list, he wrote: "I will never be a drinker like my dad because I've seen what happens when he has one too many and the rest of us suffer. I will never make condescending comments about someone's career, money problems, or weight problems like I've seen my relatives do. I will never get my kicks by making someone else feel small, which is a favorite activity among several of my relatives. I will never be rude to the guests who are invited to our family gatherings. In fact, I fully intend to make each new person at future holiday gatherings feel welcome and respected. I also plan to say something whenever my dad or another relative is insulting someone. My goal in speaking up is not to start a fight but just to say, 'That's enough. You've made your point.'"

As a result of this exercise and the other work he did in counseling, Monty gained the strength and self-confidence to have a positive voice at his family gatherings. He told me, "I just feel a lot less intimidated and not so tongue-tied around my dad and my other relatives lately. They're still the same as they were before, but something has changed inside me and I now seem to be able to find the right words to clarify who I am and what's important to me."

At first Monty's father and his other relatives responded with sarcasm each time Monty spoke up and said, "That's enough" or "Let's make these guests feel welcome." But over the next eighteen months, something began to shift in his family. As Monty commented during a follow-up session in my office, "My dad and the other family members no longer see me as a helpless victim or an easy mark for their bullying. They still sometimes roll their eyes, and every so often they still say, 'You're just too sensitive.' But their abusiveness has been reduced by 70 percent or 80 percent because they now sense I'm much better able to stand up for myself. Imagining that I'm an adult student of healthy human relationships has given me a clear sense of what I will let slide and when I will speak up and effectively set limits. My mom said recently, 'Monty, you're the first person who was ever effective at getting your father to stop hurting people. I didn't know it was possible, but you seem so clear and comfortable telling him when to lighten up, he hasn't figured out yet how to override you.'"

Creative Option #3: Look for the Wounded Soul Inside Even the Most Troublesome Family Members

This next option is an "extra credit" exercise for anyone who has some interest in spirituality, religion, or the scientific search for hidden levels of reality. But please don't think of it as an impossible task.

In fact, this third creative option is a bit like the *Where's Waldo?* books that kids love as they search for the vulnerable little face of Waldo in a collage of distracting images. However, in your family, the Waldo you are looking for is the hard-to-spot spirit of a complicated human being. In many family members, this hidden essence has been covered over by a difficult personality or a painful life history that makes it hard to see the vulnerable individual underneath it all.

Here's how to do it. If you had X-ray vision and you could look deeply into the eyes of your most difficult family member in a quiet moment, or see into this person's heart when he or she was sleeping, what would you see? Rather than being bombarded by the hostile remarks or unpleasant personality traits, for at least a moment you might be able to see the longing for love, attention, or safety that is at the root of his or her most challenging behaviors.

Or if you could find an actual photograph of this difficult relative that showed his or her innocent face as an infant, a toddler, or a young child, what might you see when you look into the eyes of that vulnerable child? You might discern the soul of a vulnerable human being more clearly than you ever could by listening to the harsh or critical comments that come out of the adult personality.

Now here's the key moment. As you look into the eyes, the heart, or the childhood soul of this complicated individual, ask yourself, "Can I connect with this person's painful longing to be cared for, to be needed, to be appreciated? Can I let go, for just a moment, of all the frustrations I have with this person and simply see him or her as a precious spirit worthy of love?"

I have seen this powerful exercise work magic in many families torn by bitter feuds and painful resentments. For example, I once counseled a woman named Luisa who had grown up feeling very resentful toward her critical and demanding mother. According to Luisa, "Just being in the same room with my mom is a painful experience. She's bossy with a terrible temper and she's forever dividing the world into loyal followers versus terrible betrayers. My mom used to feel betrayed whenever I talked to any of my boyfriends or when I had friends over and she felt left out. She had no idea how to be a good mom and also let me have a life. She was always quick to fly into a rage because she was sure I was going to turn against her the way she had turned against her own mom."

During our first several counseling sessions, I just listened supportively to Luisa as she described the verbal and emotional abuse she suffered growing up with such a fragile and explosive mom. It was the first time she'd had the chance to tell anyone the full truth about all she'd gone through. It was painful to hear just how many times her mom had jumped to the wrong conclusion or accused her of things that Luisa had not done, but it was very important for Luisa to be heard and acknowledged for being a courageous survivor of that traumatic childhood.

Then during our fourth session, I asked Luisa, "Have you ever had the chance to watch your mom during a quiet moment or when she's sleeping? Have you ever been able to see the wounded soul that is underneath all that rage and jealousy?"

Luisa looked at me skeptically. "Are you saying I should be excusing my mother's actions because she's some sort of a victim?"

"No," I replied, "and I'm glad you asked that. I truly believe that it's not about making excuses for your mom. She did some horrible things to you and she's capable of doing additional harm to you or your kids if we let her. But there's also a fragile and precious soul deep inside your mom, and it's not easy to connect with that precious soul because of all the micro-managing she does that covers it up. Has there ever been a moment when you felt drawn to her wounded soul but felt it wasn't safe because of how quickly she could snap at you and hurt you?"

As soon as I asked if Luisa had ever felt drawn to her mom's wounded soul, her eyes began to fill with tears. She took several deep breaths, then told me, "That's the biggest problem I have with my mom. On some level I do love her and I wish I could connect with her. But whenever I try to get close to her, she eventually finds a way to feel betrayed again, and she snaps at me. It's crazy-making to try to love someone who is so fragile and explosive."

Over the next several weeks, I explained to Luisa several theories of how to deal effectively with a fragile loved one who seems like a betrayal-seeking missile. Like many other people who have a parent, a sibling, a child, or a friend who fluctuates rapidly between two extremes—"I need you to drop everything you're doing and take care of me" and "I hate you because you didn't give me all that I needed, so I've decided you don't care about anyone but yourself"—Luisa felt exhausted from her interactions with her mom. Yet when we focused on this third creative option and Luisa spent some time looking silently for signs of her mom's fragile, wounded soul, something began to shift in their relationship.

Luisa told me, "I was sitting in my mom's kitchen one evening after bringing her some dinner. My mom had an achy cold and it felt positive to bring her a big bowl of her favorite soup. I was watching her take in some of the soup while she was staring out the window, lost in thought. Normally

I would have been sitting there in fear, expecting at any moment that she would start giving me advice, criticizing me, or blaming me for something. But this time my assignment was to look deeply inside my mom to see if there might be signs of a beautiful soul underneath all of her drama."

Luisa continued, "I was breathing slowly and deeply in and out, trying to stay relaxed and just watch to see if I could recognize my mom's fragile soul. For a moment, I completely forgot that this was my mom in front of me sipping the soup and staring out the window. I felt as if I were sitting next to a very delicate and beautiful child who just needed some love and some kindness. I noticed that my mother has gentle and refined hands with elegant fingers. You can also see in her eyes a sadness that feels as if it goes for miles and miles. At that moment, I felt safe and at peace with my mom. I just focused on the fact that her soul is so hungry for love and acceptance, which she never got from her own mom or from the boyfriends and two ex-husbands who abandoned her even though she's physically beautiful."

A few seconds later, Luisa noticed, "The angry and suspicious look was back on my mom's face. She started grilling me about whether I was spending too much money on organic products at the health food store and whether I had called my cousin who was recently in the hospital. She accused me of being selfish and not caring for anyone but myself. Yet even though her difficult personality was flaring up again, I still had a sense of connecting with her fragile, delicate soul. Ever since that experience of sensing my mom's deep unmet hunger for love, I don't feel as intimidated by her anxious comments or her agitated moods. Even when she's being a bit obnoxious, I still have a sense of safety and peace because I know there's a beautiful spirit deep inside this woman. I feel grateful that I've been able to bring her a bowl of soup and see underneath all her drama."

Creative Option #4: Develop a Replacement Family That Can Honor Who You Are

For some people—perhaps a quarter of the thousands I've counseled on family issues—the first three options simply don't work. In some cases, a family member has been so abusive that it's simply not safe to spend any time in close proximity to him or her. In other cases, my client absolutely needs a "sabbatical" (time off) for healing and other types of exploration and growth, before he or she can explore how to spend time with a very difficult family member whose soul is hidden deep underneath the obnoxious personality traits. That's why I support a fourth creative option that has been useful for many men and women who need time away from their families.

Every holiday season we see guilt-inducing stories on the local news and in magazines about estranged relatives reuniting after years of distance. Those who choose a temporary separation from their family face tremendous social pressure and shaming comments: "You don't even visit your own mom?" So please let me assure you that you are not a criminal if you need to respectfully say "No" a few times to the invitations (or demands) that your family tosses your way at Thanksgiving, Christmas, Hanukah, Kwanzaa, Easter, or Passover, and other events. Sometimes the only way to heal is to take time away from a toxic situation. Sometimes the only way to shake things up and take a fresh approach to your family of origin is to take one or more years off to create your own replacement family gatherings.

Here are a few brief examples of successful ways that I have seen clients deal with truly toxic family situations. See if you can read each of the following descriptions without judging the individual for choosing a non-conventional path of healing in a family that has crossed the line.

THE WOMAN WHO GRACIOUSLY EXPLAINED WHY SHE NEEDED TIME AWAY

At an all-day workshop I led on dealing with difficult relatives, I met a woman named Ariel who told me about her two-year "sabbatical" from her harshly critical family. She explained, "I told them up front in a calm, reassuring voice that this was not a punishment to them, but rather a chance for me to heal and grow so that I could one day be a part of the family again as a strong adult and not as a wounded child."

Ariel's family didn't fully understand what she was saying. "They told me I was being 'a drama queen' and 'very selfish.' Yet two years later, after a lot of therapy and great holiday gatherings with my closest friends and their families, I did feel strong enough to start seeing my own family once in a while. Those two years away from their criticism changed something inside me. The boldness of what I did in asking for a 'positive sabbatical' also got my family to realize I'm a bit unpredictable and not easily manipulated by guilt any longer. Now whenever I'm on the phone with my family or I see them in person, I can tell they are trying a little bit harder to avoid pissing me off, which I do believe is a step in the right direction."

THE MAN WHO SET UP HEALTHY ONE-ON-ONE INTERACTIONS

Several years ago I counseled Douglas, a man in his early thirties, who had been sexually abused by his uncle when he was ten. Year after year, Douglas's parents refused to believe Douglas, but kept siding with the uncle, who is quite wealthy. (Douglas's uncle is also married with four kids, has been a prominent member of his church, and has a lot of clout in the extended family.) As a result, Douglas gradually pulled away from his family.

But each year at the holidays, when he talked to friends about their holiday plans or saw ads on television featuring families gathering for warm, connected meals and conversations, Douglas felt as if the pain from his childhood was draining him of his aliveness. He also felt guilty for being the only person among his peers who had no contact whatsoever with his family of origin.

In counseling we began to explore not only the stages of recovery from a traumatic betrayal like Douglas's, but the possibility that there might be a few family members he would want to include in his adult life (especially two cousins on his mom's side who were close to Douglas in age and lifestyle). I explained to Douglas, "Yes, your uncle was abusive and your parents were unwilling to face the truth. But that doesn't mean you have to be the one to suffer forever the isolation of not having a family to connect with."

At first Douglas was reluctant to reach out to his cousins because he feared that his entire extended family might be as insensitive as his parents had been. But then he invited one of his cousins out to lunch and had a great two-hour conversation about family history and what each of them had done to stay healthy and sane in their bizarre extended family. A few months later, Douglas had lunch with the other cousin and found that she, too, was a deep and caring individual.

Douglas decided that at the next holiday, he was going to host a warm and welcoming event for several of his friends and co-workers, along with the two cousins. He told me afterward, "It was quite a triumph to be sitting there in my living room with seven people from my current life and two people from my distant past. For the first time in many years, I felt whole and complete. My uncle may have taken away some of my sense of trust and safety, but he didn't succeed in taking away my entire connection to my flesh-and-blood relatives, or my belief that there are good people even within a messed-up family."

THE WOMAN WHO HONORED HER PARENTS BY BREAKING A PATTERN

Dina came to me for counseling ten years ago, at the age of thirty-nine, after she saw on a bookstore shelf a copy of my book *The Ten Challenges*, which describes the original Hebrew meanings of the Ten Commandments and the complicated real-life dilemmas they pose. When Dina first walked into my office, she told me, "I bought your book but I can't read it yet because I'm still a bit put off by the commandment that says to honor your father and mother."

I smiled and told her, "You're not the only one. That chapter on how to honor a difficult parent is the one that brings up the most stuff for the majority of people who've used the book." Then I asked her to tell me her experience of growing up with parents who weren't very good at parenting.

In Dina's childhood, both her mom and her dad were social drinkers who became short-tempered and sometimes physically abusive when Dina talked back to them. Once her mother broke Dina's jaw; another time, Dina's father gave Dina a broken wrist. In my office, Dina looked at me and said, "How the hell do I honor these unsafe people who have never really owned up to the horrible things they did to me and to my sister?" That was the beginning of a series of conversations in which Dina and I brainstormed numerous ways to live honorably with regard to flawed parents, even if they were truly unsafe to be around (and we agreed that it would be unsafe to let them baby-sit for Dina's two young children).

Some of the ideas we came up with were:

⌘ For Dina to break the cycle of alcohol, denial, violence, and cover-ups in her family, which goes back many generations. In addition to sorting out her painful past in therapy, Dina joined a twelve-step group and became the first member of her extended family to be healthy and honest in her adult life.

⌘ For Dina to break the cycle of anger and fiery outbursts that had caused her family pain for generations. Dina took an anger management class and two parenting classes so that she could always find nonviolent and sensible ways to deal more effectively with her two high-energy children.

⌘ For Dina to be a secondary caregiver to her ailing parents as they got older. Dina felt guilty whenever her parents were ill or needed help to deal with various financial and medical problems, but she also knew in her gut that she couldn't be their hand-holder or front-line caregiver. So Dina worked closely with her younger sister, Elissa, who lives just a few blocks from their parents. Together they spoke every few months on a conference call with an excellent eldercare specialist so that they could come up with good and affordable solutions to their parents' medical problems, insurance issues, money management dilemmas, and sense of isolation. These brainstorming sessions helped Dina's parents live with dignity and comfort during their final years.

Like many people I have counseled who need distance from their toxic relatives but who still feel compassion and caring for these troubled individuals, Dina successfully came up with several creative ways to be of service without becoming trapped in the poisonous web of her family of origin. As she told me during her final counseling session, "I always thought 'honor your parents' had to be all or nothing. Either you were a dutiful martyr for your parents or you had to break away completely. But I've found it very satisfying to help in the ways I can help and at the same time to keep my life separate and healthy. My family situation is still pretty complicated, but overall I feel good at how I've been able to treat them with kindness—a lot more kindness than they often showed to me and my sister."

There are many different ways to respond with integrity and still be healthy, even if you come from a family situation that is severely troubled or unpleasant. I strongly urge you to explore your situation with a friend, counselor, sane family member, or eldercare expert in order to brainstorm various methods for dealing with one of life's toughest challenges: how do you act honorably toward someone who has not always acted honorably toward you?

I'm not recommending that you make it your job to be a roommate, best friend, or perpetual rescuer for your most difficult family members. Your job is to find the best support, solutions, and affordable help available—and not to remain a helpless victim of your upbringing.

Chapter Eight

When People Aren't Ready Yet for Your Ideas

In most Hollywood movies today, the main character reaches his or her goal successfully in less than two hours. You buy your ticket, find your seat, eat your popcorn, and leave the theater saying, "Wow, I was worried for a few moments there. But it all worked out in the end." Rarely these days does a commercial film take the risk of having an unsettled ending.

In real life, it's rarely so smooth or predictable. The complicating factors that can stand in a talented person's way are much harder to overcome. Even if you're doing everything right, there may still be obstacles and frustrations that make you wonder, "Am I barking up the wrong tree?" or "Will this good idea ever get the support it deserves?"

So if you've been frustrated lately because a decision-maker isn't returning your phone calls or a key player isn't replying to your e-mails, welcome to the club! Maybe you've got a terrific creative project that's been put on hold by people who just aren't ready for what you've envisioned. Or maybe you've come up with an exquisite idea for how to improve things in your family, at work, in your community, or at your kid's school, but certain insiders feel threatened by the changes you're suggesting. Even if your excellent new idea is much needed, it probably still faces some exasperating opposition.

How, then, do you respond effectively in situations where powerful people aren't ready to accept what you want to offer? In this chapter, I'll describe ways to stay sane and healthy even when your dreams are being squeezed by stubborn opposition. In the pages ahead, you will learn a few things about:

⌘ how to improve your chances of overcoming the delays or obstacles that are blocking your worthwhile goal

⌘ how to take care of your physical health and your emotional well-being even when you face repeated rejections and disappointments

⌘ how to decide when to keep pressing forward and when to let go of a goal that no longer has realistic potential

Suggestion #1: Get to the Truth About Whether to Give Up or Keep Going

Sometimes when a person comes in for counseling, it's clear after a few sessions that his or her goal doesn't have a snowball's chance in hell of coming true. For example, I have counseled many underemployed members of the acting, film, and dot-com industries who were very talented but couldn't find fulfillment in their overcrowded fields. Since there are over 120,000 experienced screen actors and more than 50,000 passionate people writing movie scripts, but only around 600 films get made and distributed each year, you can do the math! Clearly, some of those talented actors and dedicated writers are going to need to find other ways of paying the bills.

Or if you are one of the roughly 30,000 people trying to interest venture capitalists in your innovative website that you hope will be the next eBay, Google, YouTube, or MySpace—but you've burned through several rounds of investor money without coming up with a truly viable business plan—it might be time to find a more tangible job that has a genuine future. In a risky field like entertainment or high-tech Internet business, sometimes you have to wake up and smell the Java.

At the same time, I've counseled many men and women who were close to giving up a long-delayed dream that *was* viable, but needed just a little more persistence, networking, fine-tuning, and patience. In many of these cases, the moment of triumph didn't arrive for several more years, but it was that much more satisfying as a result of all the waiting and the extra work that had gone on in the meantime.

What about you? What projects or ideas of yours have gotten rejected or pushed aside by someone who wasn't ready yet for what you were proposing? If you have come up with a genuinely feasible plan for a business, a creative project, a nonprofit organization, or an innovation that will help and inspire people, it's important that you don't let some narrow-minded person shut you down or make you give up too soon. If you are passionate about improving some corner of the world or healing a problem that needs your unique perspective, I strongly urge you not to back down just because you've bumped up against some irritating obstacles and complications.

But how do you decide when it's time to let go and when it's time to dig deeper to keep your dream alive? To answer this question, there are two unusual methods that I've seen work wonders to restore your momentum even when you've suffered setback after setback.

THE TRUTH SERUM METHOD

To clarify whether it's time to quit or time to increase your efforts, imagine that you've taken a highly effective, completely safe truth serum. Once this amazing substance has entered your bloodstream, you are completely unable to delude yourself or anyone else. You can only tell the full truth as long as the truth serum is in your body at full strength.

In this exercise, you must ask yourself honestly while under the profound influence of the imaginary truth serum, "Do I really believe that my quest is feasible and worth the effort it will take? Am I completely willing and able to carry it to fruition? Can I be trusted to make the changes and improvements that will give this idea a greater likelihood of success?

"Or have I been less than completely honest with myself about whether this idea has what it takes to overcome the setbacks? Have I been overstating the possibilities and exaggerating the potential, maybe to drum up investors or to convince myself that it's going to work even though I have important doubts? Have I been kidding myself and others because I know deep inside I'm not fully sold on it myself?"

It's funny how the human brain works. You don't need an actual truth serum to convince your subconscious mind to tell the truth. Simply by imagining that they've taken the truth serum in this unusual exercise, most people can finally admit to themselves what is the truth. I've found that when people do this exercise with complete sincerity, they uncover some fascinating information about a goal or idea that they've been insisting is flawless; they may realize that deep inside they are unconvinced by their own sales pitch or unwilling to go the extra mile to fix a shaky concept. Or they may get new insight into necessary work that they *are* willing and able to do.

THE WOMAN WHO ASKED HERSELF TOUGH QUESTIONS

I once counseled a woman named Ginnie who was trying to decide whether she wanted to keep pursuing a long-delayed quest to improve the way art, music, dance, social skills, and personal integrity were taught at her child's school. Because of budget cuts and the "No Child Left Behind" rules, all these subjects had been eliminated from the curriculum and the teachers were under pressure to teach just what was likely to show up on the standardized tests that would determine the school's funding.

Ginnie had been trying for three years to come up with creative ways to get these subjects back into the curriculum, but she was getting nowhere. Even Ginnie's husband and several of her friends had told her to give up, saying, "The system is just not going to change" and "By the time you get any of your good ideas implemented, our kids will be grown up and out of this school altogether."

Yet when Ginnie asked herself the "truth serum" questions in my office, she learned several important things. First, she realized just how strongly she felt about the viability of her ideas and the need to keep pursuing them.

Second, she decided that even if her own kids might not benefit fully from the changes at their school, she wanted to see those changes happen nonetheless. She told me, "I think it will be a good lesson for my kids of the importance of not giving up. More important, I hope they can go back some day and visit their school with a healthy realization that these bold ideas and their mom's persistence made things better for all those who entered the school in later years."

Ginnie was also able to admit to herself under the influence of the "truth serum" that she hadn't yet done a good enough job of networking and gaining allies for the changes she wanted to make. "I think I've been a little too stubborn and independent trying to do it all myself," she said. "I need to explore the possibility that there might be other parents and even a few administrators who want to help me."

That was the beginning of an important breakthrough for Ginnie. Over the next several months, she was able to have one-on-one lunches, phone calls, and productive meetings with several parents, administrators, and community experts who agreed to make follow-up phone calls, speak eloquently at meetings, and do their part to support Ginnie's ideas. The resulting boost in teamwork and shared enthusiasm for making changes at the school led to an important series of triumphs over the next several years. A school that had refused to budge was slowly starting to change for the better.

Instead of giving up as she had been advised to do, Ginnie had become far more skillful at how to build a team of supporters for a worthwhile cause. Like many others I have counseled, she used the "truth serum" method to boost her clarity and to refine her plan for bringing her innovative ideas to fruition. (For more specific strategies for developing allies when you're perceived as a controversial outsider, please see Chapters Nine and Ten.)

THE GALILEO PERSPECTIVE

Another effective way to decide whether to give up or stay focused on a controversial idea that you care about deeply is to compare your setbacks and frustrations to those that the astronomer Galileo encountered in his own search for truth. When Galileo first put together a workable telescope in 1609 and saw three moons orbiting Jupiter, the huge fifth planet from the sun, he began to theorize that the Earth might revolve around the sun, contradicting the commonly held view that the sun revolved around the Earth. For this and other controversial insights, Galileo was arrested several times, stood trial, and was condemned by the Church in Rome as a heretic. Many of his scientific writings were banned or censored by powerful leaders who felt threatened by the enormous shift in thinking that might result from his discoveries. Galileo eventually died while under house arrest.

However, ninety-five years after his death, many powerful people were starting to realize that Galileo's ideas had been accurate. As a result, Galileo's physical remains were finally allowed to be re-interred in sacred ground. A hundred years after his death, Galileo's many banned and censored scientific writings were published in an uncensored version and made available to a wider audience for the first time.

In 1992, more than 350 years after Galileo's death, a formal inquiry into his scientific work was conducted by the Pontifical Council for Culture in Rome, after which Pope John Paul II apologized for the way the church had treated this courageous man and his innovative ideas. Today, Galileo is no longer considered a heretic or a man condemned to dishonor. He is now described most often as an archetype of perception and integrity, a human being who courageously sought to explain the mysteries of our universe.

If you're frustrated about criticism or rejection of your own creative ideas and passionate quests, and you've begun to ask yourself, "How long is too long to wait?", I can only say that I hope you get an easier journey than Galileo did. Three hundred and fifty years is a long time to wait for vindication of your good ideas.

So the next time you are watching someone in power chip away at your excellent suggestions or block your creative ideas, take a breath and say to yourself with a healthy sense of irony, "Hey, this is just starting to get interesting. I'm nowhere near giving up yet. In fact, compared to Galileo, this is a walk in the park." Seeing your personal quests not just in the current moment, but as part of a much bigger picture, will help you decide whether to give up or press on.

"MAYBE THE FIRST SEVENTEEN REJECTIONS ARE JUST A WARM-UP"

Here's a quick illustration of how to use the "Galileo Perspective" right at the moment when you are feeling upset or insecure because a passionate goal of yours is getting blocked or repeatedly rejected. This example comes from my own life.

For a number of years I had been developing some preliminary ideas for a book that I was afraid to write because it was too controversial and might provoke criticism. But even as I tried to push the ideas aside, they kept appearing to me. Whenever I was taking a long walk, when I was waking up from a dream, or when I was meditating in silence, I would repeatedly sense that this book needed to be written.

So I spent a couple of years researching and writing up a book proposal and showing it to a few people I trusted. They encouraged me to move beyond my fears and see the project through. I rewrote the proposal several times to make sure it was good enough. Then I sent it to a literary agent who had been recommended as someone courageous enough and intelligent enough to do a good job with this kind of book.

The agent said the book had great potential and submitted the proposal to six publishers he knew well. Within a few months, each of the six publishers said no. Then the agent submitted it to six more publishers. Three of these publishers nibbled, but eventually all of the second group of six said no. Then the agent submitted it to the last five publishers he thought might be interested. Two of the publishers in this group said they were very hopeful they could get their editorial boards to approve the project. But over the next few weeks, each of these five publishers backed out too, saying, "Sorry, we're not ready to do something like this yet."

During a long phone call with the literary agent, I heard the frustration in his voice as he said, "I think the message we're getting is quite clear. There doesn't seem to be a chance for this book to get published in the fear-driven climate of the book business right now. You'd better move on to another project."

So far I had spent three and a half years working on this project. I had interviewed dozens of people, rewritten the first three chapters at least ten times, and begun to envision more clearly how the book truly deserved to be written in its entirety so that it could reach the people who would benefit from it. Even a few of my most skeptical and hard-edged friends had agreed with me that this book could help a wide audience of people cope with a very important issue. But right now the seventeen rejections from publishers and the literary agent's comments were telling me in the strongest terms, "It ain't gonna happen."

So I took a long walk with my wife and we discussed whether it was worth the time and financial hardship to keep pursuing this project. I also went alone to a beautiful spot in nature not far from where we live to sit in silence and ask for guidance. In these quiet moments, I remembered the Galileo exercise that I'd done with many of my counseling clients. Suddenly I thought, "Hey, this is just starting to get interesting. I'm nowhere near giving up yet. In fact, compared to Galileo this is a walk in the park."

Two weeks later I turned up one more possible publisher and begged the agent to send the proposal to their acquisitions editor. A few months later, we received a phone call with an offer for a sizeable advance payment that led to a wonderful book that has helped tens of thousands of people. In fact, I've received more letters, e-mails, and phone calls from people about that book than about anything else I've written. It seems that even though seventeen publishers were afraid of the topic, the eighteenth publisher was willing to support a project that risked telling a controversial truth.

There's a coda to the story. Several years after that book was finally published, a client named Bertina was telling me that she had applied to seventeen graduate schools and had been rejected by all of them. She was thinking of giving up on the dream she had nurtured for many years.

Bertina looked at me with weariness and self-doubt in her eyes. "I guess it doesn't matter how passionate I am about this goal," she said. "These seventeen rejections might be telling me what I need to hear—that it's time to be realistic and move on to something else. I probably don't fit the profile of who they're looking for in these highly selective graduate programs."

I looked at this highly competent young woman and said, "Maybe the first seventeen rejections are just a warm-up. Maybe they're just a way of letting you decide if you're serious about this goal or if you're easily knocked off center." I then asked her to do the "truth serum" and the "Galileo" exercises.

Bertina's answers to the truth serum questions are what got her going again in her career. She calmly asked herself, "Can you be trusted to make the changes and improvements that will take this project to a higher likelihood of success? Or is it time to let it go?"

With these questions in mind, Bertina realized she needed to take a more rigorous test-preparation study course (and when she did, she improved her score substantially on the graduate school entrance exam). She spent several weeks working hard to clarify and refine the essays on her applications. She also showed up for her interviews with a sense of confidence and professionalism that had been missing until the seventeen rejections and the Galileo/truth serum exercises put her in the right frame of mind. I'm glad to report she was accepted to an outstanding program where she most likely will shine.

Suggestion #2: Work with Your Physical and Emotional Vulnerabilities So You Can Run a Marathon (Rather than a Sprint)

Many otherwise intelligent people start off on a difficult journey without the supplies and protection they will need to complete it. For example, at a fundraising marathon (such as for AIDS or breast cancer), you often see men and women who haven't adequately trained their muscles, joints, and lungs to go the distance. Or if you ever go hiking in the desert, you will see that some well-educated but clueless people show up without enough water, head covering, or breathable clothing to hike comfortably in the intense heat.

Please don't let that happen to you when you embark on a long, twisting journey to implement a passionate idea of yours. A great deal of self-knowledge and preparedness are required if you want to succeed with a quest that might take months or years longer than you anticipated. For example, if you want to start a successful business, launch a viable nonprofit organization, change your family's way of doing things, or make some important innovations in your church, temple, parent-teacher association, or volunteer group, you will probably need many of these essential elements:

❋ Enough cash flow, grants, loans, generous supporters, or other sources of income so that your worthy project doesn't fail for lack of funds. Research shows that the vast majority of new businesses, nonprofits, and creative projects fail not because the ideas weren't solid but because people were unable to anticipate the cash flow difficulties that arose after the initial burst of enthusiasm.

❋ Enough hands, feet, and shoulders to do the hard work required to get the job done. Many good ideas could make a difference in the world if only there were a much better organized network of volunteers or staff to bring them to fruition.

❋ Enough emotional support and knowledgeable people to consult with, so that you can hang in there longer and come up with solutions to each of the obstacles that show up along your path. Trying to do it all by yourself with no input from others is one of the surest ways to burn out. Don't jeopardize a project that requires many eyes and ears to fully address the difficulties that one overstressed person can't handle alone.

Here's an inspiring example of what it means to have the wisdom to know your own limitations so that you can be courageous enough to gather the support and resources you will need to succeed.

THE MAN WHO LOOKED CLOSELY AT WHAT OTHERS DIDN'T WANT TO SEE

How does a person with controversial ideas find the resources it takes to be recognized and appreciated in the world of powerful insiders?

The person in my own life who has taught me the most about how to achieve breakthroughs, even when the odds and the trends are stacked against you, is a good friend from college, Peter Reiss. When we first met as freshmen at Kenyon College, I sensed that Peter was a serious artist who was far ahead of the rest of us with his bold tastes in music, film, photography, and visual design. He was exploring creative photography techniques and unusual uses of video long before anyone else. While most students and faculty in the art department were trying to imitate the styles of famous artists from the past, Peter was inventing new styles that came from inside his own imagination.

What I didn't know about Peter until junior year was that he had suffered for much of his life from grand mal seizures that came on without much warning and caused him to fall to the floor and quake for minutes at a time. Doctors had given him contradictory diagnoses and different theories about what might be causing his seizures and what could be done to eliminate them.

Then, during senior year, Peter learned about an experimental surgery that had shown promising results for repairing the nerve coverings inside his brain, which seemed to be the most likely cause of his convulsive attacks. Of course, any brain surgery is a complicated endeavor, but this new procedure offered the best hope for Peter to have a healthy adult life free from seizures.

For several weeks we took long walks together near the campus as he wrestled with the difficult choice of whether or not to say yes to the surgery. Then, after much research and consultations with several experts in the field, he decided to go forward and let the doctors operate on his brain. From all the available research and the excellent track record of his surgeon, we were convinced the odds were good that the surgery would go well and reduce or eliminate the seizures.

But the surgery didn't go well at all. Peter suffered a major stroke during the operation, which paralyzed the right side of his body. And his seizures continued. He was still an artist with imaginative ideas, but to lessen the intensity of the seizures he was going to have to take very strong medications that would sometimes slow down his thinking, his speech, and his memory. In addition, he would have to walk with a cane and the near-total paralysis on his right side meant that he would hobble slowly with a pronounced and awkward limp.

Yet this wasn't the end of Peter's career as an artist; it was the spark that ignited his creativity and his persistence. In the years after his unsuccessful surgery, Peter learned how to use his left hand for eating, writing, and other tasks. He also began experimenting with a vegan diet and did intensive physical therapy to keep his energy strong and positive.

What's more, Peter learned something that many people are never able to learn—how to calmly let people know your vulnerabilities and ask gracefully for help. When he began to teach photography at art schools, he always made sure to explain to his students that he might have a seizure during class. He would appoint one or two students to make sure that he didn't knock over any chairs or desks when he was flailing on the floor and that no one shoved any wallets into his mouth during a seizure (an outdated move that supposedly keeps an epileptic person from swallowing his tongue, but in fact can do more harm than good).

As he moved on to teaching at prestigious schools like Cal Arts, Otis Art Institute, and UCLA, Peter had the humility and courage to explain his vulnerabilities to his bosses, students, and colleagues so that he could enlist their support in making sure everyone stayed calm and safe in the event of a seizure. Instead of hiding from the truth of how complicated life can be, Peter had the good sense to gently teach people how to help.

This clear-eyed view of the complicated truth—and of his own vulnerabilities—gave a new dimension to Peter's work as well. Since he had to deal with strange glances and uncomfortable whispers whenever he took a bus or walked with his severe limp in a public place, he began to focus his photography on a very personal theme. He decided to create a series of beautiful, dignified black-and-white portraits of men and women whom society doesn't feel comfortable looking at.

The first individuals Peter honored in portraiture were adults with mild or severe brain damage who were living in institutions. In another series, he showed the dignity of Alzheimer's patients and their loved ones. And he received particular acclaim for his series of portraits of men and women battling drug addiction, along with brief narratives about their daily challenges and personal pride.

Sometimes it took years of rejection slips and financial hardships before he was able to line up grants or gallery showings for one of his unusual projects. But Peter always kept eating his healthy food, staying fit with a specially designed yoga practice, and staying positive as he wrote one proposal after another until something eventually came through.

For the 1984 Olympics in Los Angeles, Peter sent in a risky but beautifully conceived plan to use an old-fashioned camera to make black-and-white portraits of the athletes who came from the poorest countries, who were least likely to win medals, and who were probably going to be ignored by the worldwide media. For several months we waited to see if the International Olympic Committee would say yes or no to an art project that didn't focus on medals but looked deeply at the human spirit. I remember vividly the afternoon when Peter got the letter saying that yes, he would receive a sizeable grant to do these portraits of the young men and women who were likely to be invisible at the upcoming games. Peter's deep and soulful pictures of these remarkable individuals inspire me each time I look at them on the walls of my home. They also command the highest prices among people who collect Peter's work.

A lot has changed in the field of brain medicine since the surgery that gave Peter a stroke and paralyzed his right side. Every few years there's a report of some new medication or advanced procedure that might be able to stop his recurring seizures. But so far there's been no breakthrough.

Still, Peter keeps getting up every morning and sending out grant proposals for the creative projects that flow from his unstoppable imagination. Expanding on his theme of bringing dignity to those whom society overlooks, Peter recently developed a series of portraits for bus kiosks throughout Southern California, funded by the City Cultural Affairs Department. One set of photos focused on the struggles of people who live with epilepsy (and included instructions posted on the kiosks for what to do, and what not to do, to help someone who is having a seizure).

HOW VULNERABLE ARE YOU WILLING TO BE?

What I find most remarkable about Peter's long unconventional career as an artist is not that he has earned critical acclaim or shown his work in galleries around the world. I believe what's even more important is that he has somehow managed to stay healthy, passionate, and productive in spite of repeated hospitalizations and the daily effort it takes to deal with his physical challenges. This fine artist may walk slowly and with a limp, but he has outlasted and outdistanced most of his speedier, trendier peers.

If you have any physical, emotional, or other personal difficulties that you've felt ashamed of or thought you had to hide, I hope Peter's story will give you more courage and freedom to be who you are. Nearly every human being is challenged with some vulnerability (as well as our own secret shame about what we think is "imperfect"). Yet from Peter's persistence and his willingness to ask for help, I have learned that it's crucial to keep your good ideas and creative visions alive and thriving no matter how many obstacles show up on a given day.

I've also learned from Peter that it's quite strong and powerful—and not at all weak or embarrassing—to look someone in the eye and say honestly, "I want to do a good job here and I have a few special needs with which I need your help."

Most of us are afraid of letting someone know we're vulnerable because we don't want to be viewed as a burden. Yet nearly all of Peter's students, employers, colleagues, and friends will tell you it's a joy and a privilege to be a part of his team and to be told from the start how to make things more accessible for him. As much as we help Peter out with the activities that his paralysis won't let him do on his own, we're helped and inspired ourselves.

Suggestion #3: Don't Measure Your Success by Immediate Results, But by Long-Term Impact

If you follow the financial news on TV or radio, or if you read the business section of your newspaper, you will often see an individual stock falling sharply on a given day because the company had a sluggish quarter or fell just a little short of their short-term projections of sales or profits. This quick-response, make-or-break reliance on key numbers might be the way things work on Wall Street, but can it measure your success as a human soul?

Ask yourself:

- ✂ If you are working on a terrific creative project that has met with obstacles or rejection, can you enjoy each small step of progress, growth, and improvement—even when the immediate results are less than you hoped and the outcome is still uncertain?
- ✂ If you are involved with a nonprofit group or another attempt to repair some part of this broken world, can you focus on the gradual progress

you are making one day at a time—even when financial concerns are flaring up and the full solution is still beyond your reach?

- If you are trying to make positive changes in your family, your work life, your relationships, or your own health, can you appreciate each good effort—even when you suffer setbacks, or feel outnumbered by people who are resistant to change?

Holding on to your positive vision for the future even when things are moving slowly in the present is essential for anyone who hears a different drummer. When we look at a great innovation, we usually think there must have been support all along for such a good idea. But in reality, good ideas are a lot like Roto-Rooter—they bring up plenty of toxic sludge while they are trying to clear out an opening.

Consider that Henry David Thoreau's brilliant visionary essays—on nonviolent civil disobedience, equal rights for all human beings, how to respect nature, how to live with greater balance, and how to develop a sustainable relationship with all of God's creations—found very little quantifiable success in the short term. Not only did Thoreau spend time in jail for his controversial beliefs, he was also the butt of jokes and disparaging comments while he was alive. Most people today don't know that the first printing of *Walden* (just 2,000 copies in all) sold so poorly that Thoreau wound up stashing most of the unsold copies on his living-room bookshelves. It soon went out of print and wasn't available in stores again until after Thoreau had died.

Yet more than a hundred and fifty years later, many thousands of people each year are still being inspired and guided by Thoreau's provocative wisdom and his personal attempts to explore a life lived in harmony with what really matters. Mahatma Gandhi and Martin Luther King, Jr., both found inspiration and strength in Thoreau's essays. Millions of people today throughout the world still quote his works on how to shape a future that respects the fragility and sacredness of all living beings. Yet if you took a snapshot of the quarterly earnings from Thoreau's ideas during his lifetime, you would probably see a flat line of indifference or a declining graph of scorn.

What about in your own life? Do you measure your success based on how much money, influence, or acceptance you've gained this year? Or are you open to the possibility that your unique vision and your positive ideas are gradually percolating through the layers of resistance, eventually leading to an outcome that will make it all worthwhile?

THE SHY WOMAN WHO IS MAKING A DIFFERENCE

I'd like to end this chapter with a true story of a woman whom I and many others have found extremely inspiring. I hope her story will give you added strength for facing setbacks, inner doubts, and sluggish results.

The woman's name at birth was Natalie McIntyre. Growing up in Canton, Ohio, she was extremely private and very shy, often teased in school for her silences and for her unusually high, raspy voice. "I had this real funny little voice," she admits, "and every time I would speak the kids would make fun of me. So I stopped talking."

A gifted student, Natalie often felt excluded socially because she was one of a very few African-American students at a highly competitive boarding school that was mostly white. She says, "Most of the kids had never been around people from other cultures. So they would say or do things that weren't always respectful. I don't think they realized it was offensive because they were never exposed to anything other than their own kind of society."

Natalie often felt a bit different in her own family as well, because her very assertive and outgoing mom, for many years a junior high school math teacher, and her dad, a strong and powerful steelworker, were so unlike Natalie's reclusive, artsy soul. During her vacations from school, Natalie's two siblings recall, "She was always writing short stories or playing solitaire and spending time in her room alone listening to music. She lived in her own private world."

Then, during a one-on-one conference with an administrator at her boarding school, Natalie recalls being surprised when the man made a sexual advance. "I was sitting there with this dean just talking and joking around, and he put his hand on my leg, like trying to feel me up."

Since she was a good student at the school, Natalie decided to speak up and report his inappropriate behavior. "My mom went up there and everything, but it was a weird place. You've got all these teachers in there just hanging around, they have all this access to young kids and the parents are far, far away. Anything can happen. It ain't really the place to be."

Though Natalie and her mom were quite specific about what had occurred, the school refused to take them seriously. Natalie got kicked out a few months later. They claim it was her poor grades. She claims it was a cover-up back in the days when uncomfortable sexual gestures from teachers were still swept under the rug.

Soon after she finished high school, Natalie decided to leave Ohio. First she applied for and won a scholarship to the United States Naval Academy. But then she chose instead to go to the University of Southern California to become a screenwriter.

Natalie's mom was shocked. She says, "I had no idea that she had even applied to USC. I told my daughter, 'What are you going to do with a screen-writing degree in Canton, Ohio? This is a Football Hall of Fame town.'"

Natalie replied, "Mom, I do not intend to live in Canton, Ohio."

Her mom later recalled, "I think she pretty much had her mind made up. And she kept it to herself, as she often did."

While she pursued her courses in writing for film, Natalie began to sing in underground clubs late at night. For a shy person, this was frightening, especially since Natalie's voice was still considered strange. But her passionate songs and her daring lyrics were memorable to anyone who heard them. To pay the bills, Natalie also took on several part-time jobs, getting hired as a production secretary for two film studios and working in a few small music clubs doing whatever tasks they needed done.

Around this time she began to use a stage name, Macy Gray, which was the name of a family friend in Canton who used to play pool with her dad and who had always encouraged Natalie's uniqueness. Despite the fact that her voice was high-pitched and scratchy, unlike any other singer's in the music business, Natalie was beginning to acquire a following in the Los Angeles club scene. So she and a few friends opened up a late-night club of their own, called We Ours, in a Hollywood coffee shop.

During the early 1990s, Natalie's unusual sound, mixing rock, soul, torch songs, standards, and rhythm and blues, created a powerful stage presence for this painfully shy young woman that knocked the socks off everyone who saw her perform. A friend of mine who happened to catch Macy Gray singing three songs at a late-night performance in 1991 said, "It was like walking into a club and seeing Billie Holiday or Janis Joplin in their pure essence, before the fame or the drugs."

Hoping that her music might be a way to make a living, Natalie decided to start sending out demo tapes and talking to people about getting a recording contract. But after three years of nothing but rejections, the artist known as Macy Gray was getting frustrated. Since no record company knew exactly what category to put her in, they kept saying, "We like your music but we can't possibly market you the way you are." Like thousands of other musicians in Los Angeles, Natalie was barely making any money from her music.

Then finally, in 1994, Atlantic Records—the company that had developed a diverse array of artists, from Aretha Franklin and Ray Charles to the Allman Brothers and Crosby, Stills, Nash and Young—signed a "new discovery" named Macy Gray. Life was looking hopeful. Natalie got married to mortgage collector Tracy Hinds, the father of her two children, who were five and six years old at the time. She went to work on her first solo album, titled *Macy Gray,* on the prestigious Atlantic label.

At first, she had some intense debates with the record company about which types of music were "this year's trends" and which songs should be cut from her album. But she was looking forward with excitement to the chance to start earning a good living and touring to reach a wide audience.

Then suddenly Atlantic Records changed its mind about Macy Gray. She was told, "We just don't know what to do with your music. It doesn't have a strong enough target market."

A few months later, when Natalie was pregnant with her third child, she and her husband separated. They later divorced. The pain of being out of work, alone with three kids, and still very shy and private was starting to take its toll on Natalie.

Unable to stay afloat in the Los Angeles music scene, Natalie moved back to live in her parents' home in Canton. She soon decided to stop pursuing her dream and enroll in classes to get a teaching certificate.

ONE MORE RISK

Almost three years later, in 1997, something strange happened. An independent music producer named Jeff Blue heard the never-released tape of Macy Gray's songs. He tracked Natalie down in Canton and for the next three months he tried to talk her into meeting him in New York for some new recording sessions. At first, she told him to get lost. "I didn't know if I could go through all the disappointments again and again," she says. But then she decided to take one more ride on the roller coaster.

Natalie and Jeff worked hard on the new demo tape and sent it out to a few contacts under a pseudonym, Mushroom, to make sure those who listened to the new songs would keep an open mind because they wouldn't connect this demo with Macy Gray and the Atlantic fiasco.

In 1998, Epic Records offered Natalie a second chance to record the deeply personal songs she'd been writing for years. In 1999, she cut her debut album, entitled *On How Life Is*. I still remember the first time I was driving in my car and I heard a completely passionate voice come on the radio—a pure unfiltered spirit that made me stop the car and say, "That was incredible. Who was that?"

The phrasing was compelling and quite unusual, combining jazz, blues, and soul rhythms. But what stuck in my mind were the heartfelt lyrics: "I try to say good bye and I choke. I try to walk away and I stumble. Though I try to hide it, it's clear. My world crumbles when you are not near." Macy Gray's unusual voice was such an eloquent cry of longing, it sounded far more genuine than any breakup song I'd ever heard.

Macy Gray won the 2000 MTV Video Music Award for Best New Artist and the 2001 Grammy for Best Female Pop Vocalist. But she still wasn't going to fit into any neat box in the music industry. Instead she has kept growing and developing as an unconventional artist and as a passionate human being. Each of her albums has taken huge risks and combined many different types of music. In a world where people are paid to stick with a "brand" that is familiar and safe for their audience, Macy Gray keeps trying bold new things. If you see her perform live, you will experience everything from call-and-response spiritual uplift and dance-rhythm hip-hop to blues, soul, pop, rock, Stevie Wonder tunes, and Bob Marley reggae.

She explains, "I'm just trying to figure out if I want to be a celebrity, or if I want to be a good underground star, or just a really talented and gifted artist. You have to make up your mind about what you want to be and honor who you are."

MAKING AN IMPACT ON FUTURE GENERATIONS

In addition to her music, Natalie has gone back to writing scripts and developing projects for film and television. She's acted in a few films and has gotten involved with several fundraising concerts where she and other musicians donate their talents. And a few years ago she established a high-quality music school for children and teens in North Hollywood. It's called the M. Gray Music Academy.

According to Natalie, "What's really interesting is how open the kids are to learning new stuff. They're way more interested in learning things they don't know as opposed to the things they've heard on the radio. Music teaches you to think differently. It's like if you go out and jog every day. Music does for the brain what jogging does for the body. It just keeps you sharp."

Can a music academy boost the creativity and personal development of teens who are living under today's enormous pressure to conform and fit in? It's far too soon to know for sure, but I've seen some terrific things happen with some of the kids who've studied with Macy Gray.

I have a close friend whose fifteen-year-old daughter is talented as a blues guitarist, but also very shy. Two years ago my friend began to car-pool her daughter to the M. Gray Music Academy. It's amazing how much this girl has expanded her world and her willingness to try new things since attending this innovative music institute. Not only has she noticeably increased her technical skill through the excellent musical education she's received, I've also seen a tremendous amount of personal growth, in part because such a respectful bond has developed between the intensely shy and sincere musical director, Macy Gray, and this intensely shy and sincere young guitarist.

When I hear stories from my friend about how gently and warmly Macy Gray connects with her own children and with each of the students at the music institute, I imagine that in the long run Natalie McIntyre's life will not be judged on album sales or show-biz awards. This true original—this vulnerable, authentic woman from Canton, Ohio—is planting seeds of creativity, strength, and courage.

I hope that the next time you hear her unmistakable voice singing, "I try to say good bye and I choke, I try to walk away and I stumble," it will encourage you in your own search for a way to make a positive impact on some corner of the world that needs your creativity and your bold new ideas. Even if you think differently from the pack mentality of others or if your ideas don't match this year's trend, I pray that your good works will reach people now and in generations to come.

Chapter Nine

How to Be an Effective Mentor, Ally, or Source of Strength for Other Outsiders

Every morning when you wake up, you have a choice. You can feel like a cranky victim living in an indifferent world. Or you can envision yourself as a vessel and know that at some point during the day you will find a way to be of service to someone who can benefit from your experience, your curiosity, or your enthusiasm.

If you could help just one person avoid the painful experience of isolation that you've gone through in the past, would you be interested? If you could assist someone in overcoming a demeaning situation at work or in a cliquish group that reminds you of something you faced a while back, would you want to reach out?

I've found in my own life, and with many of my clients, that one of the most satisfying achievements is to turn the painful parts of your own history into something healing or positive for a kindred spirit. It's remarkable when your resilience and strength can be put to good use for someone else who's going through a tough time. For some ideas about how to make this happen, consider the following:

- If you have ever been treated coldly because of your race, ethnicity, gender, sexual orientation, physical appearance, personal beliefs, or special sensitivities, what if you could prevent some of that harshness from being heaped onto someone who is younger than you and vulnerable to that kind of mistreatment?
- If you have ever felt ignored or rejected in a group situation or a family gathering, what if you could provide welcoming and support to someone who is a lot like you were?
- If you have ever been helped by someone who was an excellent mentor or ally, what if you could pass that nurturing along to someone in the next generation who might benefit from your patience and kindness?

What the Research Reveals

How much of a difference can one mentor or ally make? For the past twenty-five years, there has been a significant amount of research by psychologists and public health experts about what can spark vulnerable human beings to become more resilient and to rise above their difficult circumstances. Most of the studies point to the same factor as the key reason why some people in a tough situation stay stuck and pessimistic about their lives while others are more open to growth and finding a positive way out of even the most stressful dilemmas.

This crucial factor that has been identified for boosting human resilience is when one person truly cares and reaches out to another person who is in a vulnerable position. In one study after another, the reliable presence of a genuine mentor or ally has turned out to be the make-or-break determinant, especially for those who feel alone, cast aside, or left out during their teen and young adult years. If just one caring and persistent person shows genuine concern for this isolated individual, it creates the possibility for tremendous healing and growth.

Exploring the Hidden Realities of Helping Others

Whether in the media or at dinner parties, you've probably heard many people waxing eloquent about the joys and benefits of becoming someone's mentor. But what they don't usually say out loud is that being an effective source of support requires more than just good intentions. Not only must you follow through on your good intentions with persistence and creativity, but you may need to negotiate some sticky situations in which your good intentions can feel overbearing or patronizing to the person you are trying to help. In the pages that follow, you will learn:

⌘ what to do when a person you are trying to help is inadvertently becoming disempowered as a result of your efforts, and to assess when you need to give him or her room and encouragement to do things independently

⌘ what to do when helping someone else throws your own beliefs and certainties into question, and how to let yourself be touched and even transformed by openly connecting with someone else's world

⌘ what to do when your efforts to help someone are overloading you or draining your energy, and how to achieve a healthy balance between helping others and honoring your own struggles and priorities

To make sure that your good intentions to help a vulnerable person do all the good they can—and don't turn into unintended harm—here are some specific tips to keep in mind.

Mentoring Tip #1: Take a Few Moments Each Day to Make Sure Your Heart is Open

Some of the most amazing opportunities to help someone who has been feeling left out or excluded occur without warning. Say you're walking down the street when an anxious stranger approaches you and asks you for directions. If you are too rushed to respond to this vulnerable individual with kindness, you might unintentionally be sending out the unspoken message "You don't matter very much." Even if you have no conscious desire to do harm, your indifference will still indicate powerfully to this person that he or she is somehow unworthy. Is that what you want to be communicating?

Many years ago I heard the Nobel Prize winner Desmond Tutu speak about growing up in South Africa under apartheid, where his brown skin meant his opportunities in life were supposed to be severely restricted. Someone in the audience asked him, "Why did you choose to become a priest in the Anglican Church, which is made up of the same people as those who are part of the oppressive ruling class?"

Desmond Tutu smiled and replied calmly, "That's very easy to answer. When I was a young child I saw a white man tip his hat to a black woman. Please understand that such a gesture was completely unheard of in my country. The white man was an Anglican bishop and the black woman was my mother."

That one vivid memory was the beginning of a lifelong connection between young Desmond Tutu and a religious group that he could easily have assumed would exclude him. Yet he not only chose to become a member of that particular denomination, he eventually became the revered archbishop of his nation.

Is it possible that just one sincere moment of opening your heart—an act as simple as showing genuine respect to a stranger—can become a life-changing breakthrough, not only for one family but also for an entire society? It makes you wonder what unintended impressions you and I are creating each day in the way we treat the strangers we encounter, or even in the way we treat a friend or a loved one who is feeling alone.

Yet since most of us are very busy people, exactly how do we stay open and receptive when we're approached by strangers, acquaintances, students, co-workers, colleagues, or friends who need our help? How can we find the extra energy to come through with warmth and respect on a stressful day rather than responding coldly "I'm just too busy" to the unexpected requests we receive to stop what we are doing and pay attention to someone else's basic humanity?

This can be most difficult at the end of a frustrating or over-filled day when your spouse, child, roommate, or other loved one is in need of some good listening from you. Maybe you were hoping to tune out the world that evening with your favorite television show, a book, or a drink to take the edge off. Yet is it possible that if you take a relaxing breath in and out, you might have a few additional minutes of deep compassion left in your heart? Or are you going to say to your loved ones those famous dismissive words, "Cut to the chase," "Get to the point," or "Hand me the remote"?

THE OVEREXTENDED SUPERMOM

Here's an illustration of what I mean by finding the extra energy to keep your heart open to the outsiders in your midst. It's the story of a hard-working creative woman named Birgitta who was juggling several tough situations in her life when she was referred to me by her internist because of her stress-related physical symptoms. See if her story sounds like you or someone you know.

During the first session in my counseling office, I heard from Birgitta just how much she was able to cram into her busy daily schedule. She looked weary as she described how she had been trying for several months to help her husband, who had carpal tunnel syndrome. Birgitta was handling the family bills, dealing with stubborn insurance companies, and driving her husband to physical therapy appointments so he could learn how to do his graphic design work with less stress on his wrists and elbows.

She had also been doing a lot to help their two kids—their fourteen-year-old son, who needed daily assistance with his asthma, and their eleven-year-old daughter, who required enormous patience and attention to deal with the daily homework assignments that stirred up tensions because of her learning disabilities.

In addition, Birgitta had been running her own florist business for several years and was now training a young woman, a refugee from Chechnya, as her part-time assistant. Each day the combined jobs of wife, mother, tutor, driver, boss, mentor, and supportive ally were piling an increasing load on Birgitta's shoulders.

She told me near the end of our first session, "Living with a lot of chaos is nothing new for me. I grew up in a home where there were lots of arguments and both of my parents became short-tempered when they drank too much, which happened at least once a week. While most of the kids at my school were out having fun and feeling carefree, I was stuck in the role of trying to calm down my parents, who were often hammered and liable to get on each other's nerves."

As an adult, Birgitta worked hard to avoid alcohol and build a successful family life and career. But she admitted, "It still feels like a huge uphill climb sometimes. There are mornings when I wake up exhausted and nights when I simply can't unwind because of how much I handle each day. So when my husband or my kids get in a foul mood or they don't help out around the house, I sometimes feel like I'm at the end of my rope and that I've got nothing left to give."

Like most of us who wear many hats and want to come through for all the people who depend on us, Birgitta was beginning to wonder, "Is it possible to be strong for everyone else when I'm starting to feel overloaded myself?"

A previous therapist, a thrice-divorced man in his sixties who was largely focused on lowering his golf score and avoiding attachment, had advised Birgitta to "stop being so involved in so many stressful situations." This self-involved therapist (whose three ex-wives have stories that would make your jaw drop) told her, "You just need to toughen up and say no to all these people who magically think they can depend on you."

But Birgitta had decided that cutting herself off from people she cared about was not a good answer for her. She stopped going to the other therapist because, as she put it, "I need to find some way to be more effective in helping the people I care about deeply, while at the same time staying balanced and healthy myself. There's got to be a way to become a more effective parent and caregiver for my loved ones without becoming burned-out or impatient."

To help Birgitta find additional energy and keep her heart open to everyone who looked to her for strength, we addressed three specific issues. First, we explored the pressure and the frustrations she had experienced as the highly competent child of alcoholic parents. Birgitta made enormous progress in therapy at sorting out what she liked and what she resented about growing up quickly and being the responsible one when her parents couldn't deal with their own mood swings and drinking binges. She also learned how to ask for help in an effective way and to get better teamwork from her husband and her children.

Second, I showed Birgitta a few acupressure self-massage techniques she could do at home, at work, or while sitting at a red light; when she used them, she experienced a noticeable decrease in her stress and a substantial increase in her patience and resilience. For many years I'd studied acupressure and other helpful mind-body methods with various teachers and found, in my own life and with many of my clients, that these techniques were quite powerful for preventing burnout and increasing energy levels, especially for people who were handling a lot in their daily lives. In Birgitta's case, she got a huge boost in her sense of calmness and strength when she used her thumb to press for thirty seconds on the notch at the side of the opposite hand, just underneath the knuckle that sits below the little finger. You can try it yourself, applying five seconds of steady pressure below the side of the knuckle of the fifth finger on one hand, then doing the same to the notch just below the knuckle of the baby finger at the side of the other hand. She also felt revived and less stressed when she massaged the cushiony pads on the sides of each of her ten fingertips firmly for a few seconds each, a few times a day.

Birgitta told me, "I had always assumed that it was going to require at least a fourteen-day vacation or a spa getaway weekend for me to unwind from all the stress in my life, neither of which I can afford to do right now. But these simple acupressure techniques in just a minute or two a few times a day give me a surprisingly strong sense of relief and renewal exactly at the moments when I need them the most."

Finally, I explored with Birgitta how to adjust what she said to herself about her efforts to help others. Like many caring and devoted people, Birgitta often felt frustrated when her efforts to help her husband, her kids, or her employee couldn't resolve all the difficulties in their lives.

"No matter how much I do for each of these four people that I care about," she explained, "they each still have difficulties that I can't prevent. So I'd often end up with a hopeless feeling that no matter what I did, it was never enough." We realized this was very similar to the feeling of hopelessness she experienced as a teenager, when nothing she did could make her parents stop drinking or fighting with each other.

To overcome this sense of hopelessness and burnout, we explored a different type of self-talk. Instead of repeatedly saying to herself, "No matter what I do, it's never enough," Birgitta began to experiment with phrases that were far more honest and realistic. The two sentences that worked best for her (and for many of my counseling clients) were: "I'm doing a lot and I'm fortunate to be able to help others. I deserve to breathe right now and feel good about the fact that I'm making a small but significant difference for each of these people I care about."

These two sentences, comforting but accurate, sound simple enough. Yet if you repeat them to yourself silently during stressful moments, you will be surprised at how they begin to change the way you feel about your efforts to help.

Some clients put these words (or another phrase the client comes up with) on a note card that he or she keeps where it's easy to find exactly at the moments when this kind of support is needed. Birgitta wrote the words on a small sticky note that she taped to the back of her cell phone, and she looked at it carefully during stressful moments for the first few days. Then she memorized the two sentences and began to say them silently from her heart whenever she was feeling overburdened or discouraged.

Now she says, "Whenever I start to feel impatient because my husband isn't doing all the exercises his physical therapist wants him to do, or when my daughter is putting up a fuss about her homework, I stop and take a deep breath. Then I quickly relax my entire body with two or three minutes of acupressure massage. While I'm doing that, I say calmly to myself, 'I'm doing a lot and I'm fortunate to be able to help others. I deserve to breathe right now and feel good about the fact that I'm making a small but significant difference for each of these people I care about.'

"Each time I do these things, I get a noticeable burst of renewed energy. It's as though the acupressure and the supportive self-talk take me deeper to a place inside me where there is more strength than I ever knew I had access to."

Using these tools and taking charge in this manner has helped Birgitta consistently to keep her heart more open, even on very busy and stressful days. Like many of my clients, she has found that the greatest satisfaction comes not from turning away from your responsibilities, but from engaging fully in life with a deeper sense of inner strength and clarity.

Birgitta told me recently, "I realize I'm still doing a lot each day to help other people, which I'm sure the golfing therapist with the three ex-wives would call 'co-dependence.' But for the first time in my life, it feels very good because I've got more than enough energy to deal with all the stuff that's on my plate. In fact, on most days when I'm putting together beautiful floral arrangements and teaching this young woman from Chechnya how to be successful in business, I feel enormously grateful just to be alive. It's quite different from the burned-out, impatient, resentful way I used to feel, and I'm starting to see that I'm a lot more effective now with my son, my daughter, and my husband, too."

Mentoring Tip #2: Know When to Give Someone Room to Rebel

One of the problems we run into when we're trying to guide someone in a tough situation is that he or she doesn't always do what we believe is best for him or her to do. We may have some good ideas on how to help someone, and we hope the other person will go along with our good ideas, but this unique individual clearly has a mind of his or her own. Or maybe the other person acts rebellious or defiant and we take it personally.

Has that ever happened to you? Have you seen any of these warning signs that your "help" is starting to feel overbearing or uncomfortable to the person you were hoping would deeply appreciate your kindness? Ask yourself:

- ✄ Has the person you were trying to help ever acted defiant or resentful toward you, even when you were doing something kind or supportive?
- ✄ Does this person ever reluctantly agree to let you do something for him or her, but with an unspoken feeling of sadness, resignation, or loss of control that you can sense (but that he or she is too polite or too afraid to articulate)?
- ✄ Has this person ever been impatient or quick to disagree with your suggestions, as if saying, "I don't like being told what to do"?

If this sounds like a subtle battle for control that you have experienced with someone you're trying to help, don't put yourself down. You probably didn't mean to come on too strong; it's never easy to find the right balance between how much to get involved in others' daily lives and how much to back off and let them find their own way to do things.

Instead, if you discover you're being a tiny bit too meddling toward someone who is resisting or resenting your help, here are a few effective ways to break the cycle.

- ⌘ *Say humbly to the other person that you need to know when your help is working and when it's not.* You might say something like, "I need your help to teach me when I'm being useful to you and when I'm being an unintentional irritant because I'm making it harder for you to do things your own way. Please let me know which things you want me to do for you, which things you want me to let you do on your own, and which things you want to do mostly by yourself with just a little bit of support when you request it."
- ⌘ *Make sure to ask every so often about what else is unspoken between the two of you.* You could say, every third or fourth time you see this person, "I'm hoping we can be real with each other and not just be polite. So let's take a few minutes and clear up any awkward moments or miscommunications that have happened lately."
- ⌘ *Brainstorm to come up with a playful signal that says you've overstepped.* Maybe you've underestimated what this person prefers to do without any assistance or interference from you. Open up the conversation by suggesting that the two of you come up with a nonverbal signal that the person you're supporting can use whenever he or she senses you're trying too hard or stepping on his or her independence.

THE TUG OF THE EARLOBE

Burt is a caring and helpful person by nature. He's worked in various high-powered jobs as a human resources executive, and he's also active in a nonprofit group that mentors teens and young adults who live in tough neighborhoods.

Burt tries hard to be of service to the many employees he deals with in his job and to the young man named Juwann whom he mentors by phone two nights a week and sees in person one weekend a month for three-hour field trips. Burt considers his work with Juwann, who is fourteen, one of the most important parts of his busy life.

Yet Burt admitted to me during one of our sessions, "I sometimes get the feeling that Juwann is irritated with me about something, but he doesn't come out and tell me what it is. In fact, during the past few weeks Juwann has been a bit sarcastic and rebellious with me on the phone and in person. I'm concerned that he's getting tired of the whole mentor thing and I'm worried he's going to do something to jeopardize our working together."

I asked Burt, "If you were Juwann, what might be the subtle thing that gets on your nerves about this mentor fellow named Burt?"

Burt thought for a moment. "If I were in Juwann's shoes, I'd be pissed off that this know-it-all adult comes into my world every now and then with all this helpful advice and pep talks, yet the bottom line is that we live in different universes. I'd also be frustrated at how Burt does all sorts of favors for me without asking anything in return. If I were Juwann, I'd be thinking, 'Burt must think I'm a pathetic hardship case,' and I'd resent being patronized like that."

As soon as Burt finished saying what he would resent if he were Juwann, sadness came into his face. "What an awkward situation this is," he said. "I'm trying to help Juwann by being his mentor with homework and talking about his personal life and going on these weekend outings. Yet from Juwann's perspective, I'm just reinforcing the fact that he's in desperate need of help and that he's always one-down to me in our conversations. And since Juwann is so quiet and soft-spoken, he's probably not comfortable telling me when I've made him feel patronized."

This insight was the beginning of an important change in Burt's way of interacting with Juwann. I suggested that Burt have a talk with Juwann to give him equal power to direct their interactions and be more of a co-leader than he'd been in the past.

I said to Burt, "Ask Juwann to come up with a nonverbal signal that will clue you in each time an interaction with you starts to feel patronizing or uneven. Instead of just 'putting up with' your intrusive helpfulness, let's give him a chance to safely signal you that it's starting to feel excessive."

Over the next few weeks, Burt discussed with Juwann how they needed to be two creative co-directors figuring things out together, rather than one know-it-all adult and one passive kid. And Burt did ask Juwann to come up with a playful nonverbal signal to use each time their relationship felt unbalanced.

Juwann smiled at that suggestion and pulled on his right ear lobe. He said, "I'll let you know each time you get on my nerves. Deal?"

That playful signal significantly changed the way the two interacted. Juwann became a lot less rebellious and a lot more involved in guiding their activities and their topics of conversation.

"Now whenever Juwann reaches up and pulls on his right ear lobe," Burt says, "he gets this playful mischievous look on his face and our time together becomes so much richer and more creative."

THE DISCIPLINED STUDENT WHO NEEDED TO BURST OUT

When someone you're trying to help becomes rebellious or agitated, it's not always because you've been "too helpful." This person may have spent years being coached or prodded by so many authority figures and as a result the situation has reached the boiling point where he or she feels like exploding.

I've always been impressed by the musical skills and warm personality of the talented cellist Yo-Yo Ma. But what I didn't know until recently is how, at an earlier time in his life, he had to rebel against the strict discipline and the intense expectations imposed on him. His story is a great example of why a mentor has to give some breathing room to those he or she is trying to help—and how that breathing room can be the most important breakthrough in this person's life.

Yo-Yo Ma was an outsider from the time he was born, as one of the few Asian children living in Paris in the mid-1950s. His father was a music scholar and violinist from Shanghai with a job teaching music. His mother was a talented singer from Hong Kong. His older sister was a violinist, too.

While most of the French kids in his neighborhood were playing outside and making friends, Yo-Yo Ma was rehearsing some of the most difficult music in the classical repertoire. At the age of five, he gave a concert at the University of Paris and stunned the audience with his talents. When he was seven, the family moved to New York City, where the young boy continued to impress people with his discipline and his mastery.

Yet by the time Ma graduated from high school, something began to stir inside him. At a music camp in the Adirondacks, the teenager turned rebellious. He admits, "I just went wild, never showed up at rehearsals, left my cello out in the rain, beer bottles all over the room, plus midnight escapades to go swimming, and just about everything. The news of my drinking spread to people who knew my family in France. All I was trying to do was to be accepted as one of the guys and not considered a freak."

His mentor, a highly disciplined cello teacher named Leonard Rose, knew instinctively that this burst of rebelliousness might be a good thing for the young musician. "I'm embarrassed when I think of the language I used," Ma recalls. "But Mr. Rose took it in his stride and saw me through this phase. At some level he must have been very happy to find me opening up in that way. Which was very fortunate, because at that point I was well on my way to being a very restricted, cautious, neurotic musician who was losing all my joy for playing."

This explosion of creative freedom became a key to the rest of Yo-Yo Ma's life. Instead of being just a virtuoso who stays within well-defined classical boundaries, he has continually gone into uncharted areas to explore new ways of inspiring people with his cello. With a boundless curiosity and a love of different genres, Ma has collaborated on projects with innovative vocalist Bobby McFerrin, singer-songwriter James Taylor, jazz pianist Claude Bolling, Appalachian folk and bluegrass musicians, and Brazilian dance experts.

He's inspired audiences with joyous and unconventional cello arrangements in places as formal as the White House and as informal as *Sesame Street, Mister Rogers' Neighborhood,* and New York City sidewalks. He's created an entire traveling company of musicians of many different ethnicities, called the Silk Road Project. These musicians work as a team to research, rediscover, and create new arrangements of rarely heard cultural masterpieces from the nations along the ancient trade routes from Italy to

China, bringing to new audiences all over the world the joyous sounds of Turkey, Pakistan, India, Persia, Uzbekistan, China, and other cultures of Central Asia.

Because he was fortunate to be guided by mentors who let him break the rules and defy what people thought he should be, Yo-Yo Ma has devoted his adult life to helping other musicians burst out of confining boxes and explode expectations of the kind of music a person is allowed to enjoy. As one Silk Road Project colleague commented, "He has taken the most neglected folk songs and instruments of many diverse cultures and made them come alive again with his splendid virtuosity. The whole world of music is more closely connected now because of how he has supported and encouraged the creativity of so many different musical colleagues."

Mentoring Tip #3: Be Willing to Have Your Cherished Views Shaken Up

Sometimes when you least expect it, a person you are trying to help will suddenly challenge you in ways that are extremely beneficial. Even if you thought your role was to be lifting up this person, in fact this person will be lifting you up. But you need to be open to these unexpected moments of awakening.

I once counseled a reading specialist named Eugene who spent many years trying to prove that his way of helping kids and adults to overcome dyslexia was superior to the methods being used by other experts. Like many hard-working people in the competitive world of university professorships, research grants, and government funding, Eugene was constantly writing papers, giving talks, and training interns in how to use his particular method for teaching people with learning disabilities to read more fluently and with better comprehension.

Then one day he told me about an eleven-year-old girl who had been sent to him by a local school district because she didn't respond at all to Eugene's highly regarded approach as taught by one of his trainees. The school district wanted Eugene to work with her personally.

After several sessions in which the girl continued to show no progress, Eugene told me, "This doesn't make sense. This girl is either being stubborn or she's just not teachable whatsoever."

I asked Eugene, "Do you really believe in your heart that this girl is incapable of learning how to read?"

He replied, "I've done everything I know how to do and it's not working. It's frustrating and I'm not a very patient person."

"What if you weren't the founder and marketer of a particular reading method?" I asked. "What if you were just a creative guy who was going to improvise with this individual to see what worked for her? What do you think might happen?"

Eugene looked a bit uncomfortable. He said, "That's asking me to do something I haven't done for many years. When I first started out as a reading mentor with no training, it was all about being creative and improvising. That's essentially how I developed the method that has proven so successful. But now it's a completely different time in my life. I've got hundreds of people—employees, educators, consultants, marketing staff—who depend on me to defend this method against all competitors. I can't start acting as if the method is in need of a revision."

I nodded my head in agreement. "You're right. It's a huge responsibility to protect all the years and efforts that went into the current method."

Then I said to Eugene, "But we still need to find an answer to the question of what you want to do to help this eleven-year-old girl who desperately wants to read. You are a talented reading specialist. Are you willing to be in a brainstorming, open frame of mind again—to use your creative insights and explore with her a new variation or combination of methods that might make reading less stressful? Or do you plan to give up on her?"

Eugene smiled. "I do like a good challenge. No question about it. So count me in for going a few more rounds to see what might work with this girl. I don't know the answer yet for her, but I do know how to be creative and explore some new possibilities."

Over the next few months, Eugene began to improvise with this child to find out what might help her break into the world of fluent reading. Eugene tried some unconventional methods, and he checked in every few minutes with an open mind to see what this young girl was remembering well and what was making it harder for her.

After a few hopeful sessions where Eugene saw signs of improvement, he began to piece together a new, better combination method for helping the hard-to-reach child. This new method not only made a difference for this one particular girl, it became the start of a whole new set of improvements in Eugene's method. Several thousand other children and adults have benefited from this improvisational research that Eugene did with this girl. As a result, Eugene has begun to put the joy back into his stressful career.

Eugene told me, "I was beginning to feel like a defensive guardian of a stale method that had no flexibility whatsoever. Now I'm feeling alive again because each day I'm learning more about how to refine and improve the method for the sizeable percentage of kids who don't fit the mold. It makes me feel twenty years younger and a lot more creative than I've felt in a long time."

Are You Stuck in a Narrow Rut?

Like Eugene, most of us get attached to one way of doing things, and it's hard to open up and improvise when the person you are trying to help might need something different and new. But if you're willing to have your cherished ideas challenged, everyone can benefit. If you want to be a more effective mentor or ally to someone who's been having a difficult time fitting in, you may need to go through the uncomfortable phase of "not knowing" that Eugene went through. For example:

※ If you're a manager or supervisor at work and you're trying to help a worthwhile employee, colleague, or customer who simply doesn't fit with the "way we do things around here," are you willing to explore some new and unusual ways of getting the job done? Are you willing to brainstorm with this individual and with others who are open-minded, asking, "How do we create an environment that welcomes and encourages original ideas and different perspectives? How do we make sure no one gets shunned or ignored when he or she raises a legitimate concern or offers a bold new idea?"

⌘ If you're a scientist or researcher in the biological, physical, or social sciences who gets caught up in the currently prevailing paradigm, what can you do to support and encourage an exploration of the anomalies, exceptions, and divergent data that might indicate a possible shift? Who in your group of colleagues, supervisors, and staff might be your allies in creating an environment where curious questioners and expansive thinkers are encouraged and rewarded (rather than being shunned or punished for thinking outside the current trends)?

⌘ If you're running your own profit or nonprofit organization, or working as a sales or marketing professional, do you ever find yourself trying to push an outdated solution on your customers and clients, even though you sense in your heart that your approach needs to be revised or improved? Do you ever get into arguments with your staff or your customers when they try to make your product more user-friendly? Or are you open to hearing what they truly need and then designing a combination of solutions that addresses their particular situation?

⌘ If you are a healer, counselor, health professional, parent, or educator, have you found a way to respect the diversity of the unique individuals you are trying to help—whether they're your patients, your students, or your children—and listen to what they have to say? Or do you find that you sometimes alienate a certain hard-to-reach person because you are so rushed or impatient that you don't make room for this person to teach you what he or she truly needs?

THE DOCTOR WHO LET HERSELF BE MOVED AND CHALLENGED BY HER OWN PATIENTS

Let me tell you about the unusual woman who first taught me the importance of listening patiently and being willing to have your long-standing ideas transformed by someone you are trying to help. Her name was Dr. Elisabeth Kübler-Ross. I was twenty-five years old when I enrolled in a Ph.D. program where she was teaching, and I'm extremely grateful for what I learned from her. I hope her story will be useful for you and anyone you are seeking to help.

Born in Switzerland as the eldest of triplet girls, Elisabeth weighed only two pounds at birth and the doctors weren't sure she would survive. Even though she was always small for her age and her health was fragile at times, this sensitive woman soon became a strongly independent thinker.

In her conservative, traditional family, she was expected either to be an assistant in her father's office supply company or to go to work as a maid in rich people's homes. But Elisabeth defiantly insisted that her calling in life was to be a doctor and help people.

In her medical studies, Elisabeth was told repeatedly that the role of the doctor was to stay "scientific and detached" toward the patient. Yet she knew from her own experiences as a pediatric hospital patient and as a caregiver for various friends and relatives that the more she listened to the needs and feelings of each patient, the better she could find the way to help each unique individual. But she also knew that it was considered unprofessional and unscientific to listen too closely to what a patient or a family caregiver requested. After all, the doctor was the ultimate authority.

When Elisabeth became a country doctor in her native Switzerland, she hoped she would be able to spend time talking with her patients not only about their symptoms but about the emotional ups and down of their recovery process. But then she married an American medical student, moved to New York, and began to work in large urban hospital settings. She was warned several times by supervisors that she needed to learn to fit in and stop spending so much time with each individual patient.

In addition, Dr. Kübler-Ross discovered a few painful realities about the medical profession that upset her deeply and made her feel like even more of an outsider. First, she realized that medicine has its limits, that not every illness can be cured in every circumstance, and that medical schools wouldn't talk about what to do when an illness was not responding to any existing treatment.

Second, she saw repeatedly that doctors were being forced—through raises, bonuses, firings, and daily criticism—to be brusque, cold, and efficient with their patients. Her supervisors made it clear that being a "good doctor" meant there was never going to be time to simply listen to what the patient was going through on an emotional level, on a spiritual level, or in terms of family concerns. In her performance evaluations and interviews for new positions, Elisabeth was told that if she didn't start becoming more "efficient," her future as a doctor would be limited.

Third, she witnessed many instances in which doctors actively lied to patients. If a cancer patient who had run out of possible treatments asked, "Am I dying?", the doctor would usually reply, "Don't be silly" or "How could you think something like that? Be strong!" Elisabeth thought that she would have to break the rules on her own; she'd just be careful not to get caught being truthful with patients who were asking important questions.

Then a strange thing happened. Dr. Kübler-Ross was working at a hospital in Denver when her supportive mentor, Dr. Sydney Margolin—a riveting speaker whose lectures to the medical staff and students were always well-attended—told her that he was going to Europe for several weeks. When Margolin asked her to take over his lectures at the medical school, Elisabeth was surprised and terrified. She recalls, "This wasn't just an honor; it was an impossibility. Professor Margolin was a colorful, animated speaker whose lectures were more like performances, intellectual one-man productions. They attracted the largest audiences in the school. How could I step into those shoes? When it came to speaking in front of groups, large or small, I was terribly shy and insecure. 'You have two weeks to prepare,' he said. Then he added, 'I don't follow a syllabus. If you'd like, look through my files. Pick any topic you want.'"

For the next week, Elisabeth went to the medical library during every free moment and tried to find a topic on which she could fill two hours. She considered and then rejected a number of topics. Then she asked herself, "What do future physicians need to know? What might help doctors who are too detached in their approach to patients? What could help them confront the simple, down-to-earth feelings, fears, and defenses that people have when they enter the hospital?"

A few days later an idea popped into her head. She imagined that during her first two-hour lecture to the future doctors, she would talk about death. She remembers reflecting, "Every patient and doctor thinks about it. Most fear it. Sooner or later, everybody has to confront it." It was something doctors and patients had in common, and it was probably the greatest mystery in medicine. It was also the biggest taboo.

But could she, with her fear of public speaking, possibly talk about something so risky in front of a large audience of skeptical, detached doctors and medical students? Would she be making a huge career mistake? Or could she help doctors become more comfortable dealing with death if they understood it better, if they simply talked about what it was like to die?

While she was anxiously trying to decide whether or not to talk about this forbidden topic, she happened to be walking through the hospital doing rounds, and she spent time listening to a sixteen-year-old girl named Linda, who was dying of leukemia. Dr. Kübler-Ross had talked with Linda several times about how frustrating it was for Linda that her doctors were cold and impersonal toward her, that Linda's parents kept pretending everything was going to be fine, and that the mail she received from friends and neighbors was always so upbeat, hopeful, and inaccurate.

Only with Dr. Kübler-Ross could Linda pour out her feelings. Only the young woman doctor from Switzerland could listen well enough to let this sixteen-year-old leukemia patient talk about what it was really like facing death alone in a cold hospital where no one else was willing to discuss her profound questions, frustrations, and fears. After a beautiful heart-to-heart conversation about what Linda needed in order to make sense of her complicated situation, Kübler-Ross felt as if this young woman had great wisdom that needed to be heard.

So she asked Linda to come and speak to the doctors and medical students with her. Dr. Kübler-Ross explained in her memoirs many years later, "Linda fascinated me, this brave girl, and I knew the medical students had to hear from her. 'Tell them all the things you could never tell your mother,' I urged. 'Tell them what it's like to be sixteen and to be dying. If you are furious, get it out. Use any kind of language you want. Just talk from the heart and soul.'"

That two-hour lecture, which touched on the various emotional stages a person goes through when facing a serious diagnosis and described what it feels like to face death, captivated the audience. It became the first of many brilliant talks that Kübler-Ross put together in order to teach caregivers what a patient deeply longs for when going through a serious illness. And it laid the groundwork for Dr. Kübler-Ross's seminal work on the stages of grief.

These lectures became the beginning of a major revolution in the medical profession and in society as a whole. Elisabeth spent the next seven years researching thousands of cases to find out exactly what men and women think, feel, and desperately need from their doctors, nurses, family members, friends, and caregivers. She uncovered the secrets and the private longings no one had been willing to discuss. She found out precisely what helps people deal more effectively with serious illness and what causes them to be confused, isolated, or to shut down.

Her research and lectures eventually were turned into a book with the deliberately provocative title *On Death and Dying,* which, to the surprise of many, became a huge international bestseller. Kübler-Ross's writings and talks over the next few decades sparked profound changes in how the world views the emotions surrounding a frightening diagnosis, how to improve honesty between doctors and patients, and how to establish better end-of-life care and counseling. The hospice movement to create a dignified and compassionate setting for people to complete their time on earth grew enormously as a result of the teachings of Kübler-Ross and others. Tens of millions of men and women have been able to talk to their loved ones more openly about important issues because of the deep listening that Elisabeth Kübler-Ross has taught in her courses, books, articles, tapes, and workshops.

I don't expect that most of us will ever have the worldwide impact that this small and fragile woman had during her lifetime. But I do hope that each of us will be inspired by her willingness to listen to even the most forbidden and uncomfortable issues that come from the heart and soul of those she tried to help.

Because of Elisabeth Kübler-Ross, we all have learned it's important to be a little less rushed and a lot more open to hearing the deepest fears and concerns of those who are being ignored or cast aside because of a physical ailment. Her books and tapes are filled with specific examples of how to tune out your own insecurities and instead tune in to the profound feelings and issues that people can reveal to you if they trust you are fully present and caring.

I vividly remember what it felt like as a twenty-five-year-old to be talking one-on-one with this unusual woman and hearing her gentle Swiss accent. Unlike many experts who are constantly talking *at you* and making you feel one-down and weak, Elisabeth Kübler-Ross would embrace you calmly with her eyes and her caring presence, while urging you to express any disagreements or opposing views you might have. Despite her busy schedule and her many awards and accomplishments, she could open up her heart and be fully present no matter what was being expressed—anger, rage, concerns, sadness, confusion, joy, playfulness, curiosity, stubbornness, hopefulness. Countless people experienced breakthroughs in their own healing and sense of peace as a result of talking with this amazing listener.

I urge you, the next time you are face-to-face with someone who sees things differently from you, to take a moment to breathe and allow your view of the situation to be shaken up a bit by the person who is offering a new set of ideas. It takes a deep curiosity and a profound respect for the dignity of every human being, but if we build upon the insights of each person who has something to contribute, we discover profound solutions that could not have been seen from our own narrow perspectives.

Mentoring Tip #4: Hold a Positive Vision of the Person You Are Helping, Even When He or She Has Lost Sight of His or Her Own Value

There's one more way to improve your effectiveness as an ally. It's about the delicate situation of assisting someone who simply cannot see his or her own true potential.

Maybe this person has been criticized or shamed by important people in the past, so your words of encouragement cannot penetrate the low self-image that covers his or her mind like a cloud. Possibly he has been praised or pumped up in the past by people who were full of hot air, and as a result the trust is gone. Or perhaps, sadly, she had others who encouraged her in the past, but when she disappointed those supporters, the will to keep trying began to slip away.

In any case, it's going to take a lot of strength on your part to hold on to your positive vision of this person's potential. Even if no one else is willing to believe in this individual, you can be the stubborn advocate who doesn't give up.

I'll end this chapter with one example of what can happen if just one person continues to believe in a unique individual who has lost faith in himself or herself.

THE ANGRY KID WHO COULDN'T STOP TALKING

In East Los Angeles, there was a young Mexican-American boy who called himself Tony Villar. His early years made it look highly unlikely that he would ever amount to much. His troubled dad, who used to beat up on Tony and Tony's mom, also got involved in several street fights; he left the family when Tony was five years old.

With his devoted mom's encouragement, Antonio (as he is now called) worked hard in middle school and was hoping to do well at the prestigious private Catholic school, Cathedral High, that she had picked out for him. But then a benign tumor in his spine during his sophomore year required surgery and left him paralyzed for several weeks.

Antonio was angrier than ever. His grades dropped and he began to alienate the school administration because he got into fights and he led a student walkout that became a public relations nightmare for the school. Then after another fight, Antonio got kicked out.

He transferred to Roosevelt High, a public school that had a much tougher student body. At Roosevelt, this short, hyper young man became even more frustrated because he was forced to take vocational classes he considered boring and limiting.

His friends knew he was very smart, and they also knew he could talk up a storm. In fact, several of his friends later told how "Tony rap" was an excellent resource whenever they took a long car ride. With his high-energy personality and his tendency to talk your head off, Antonio could keep any driver awake all night.

With lots of energy and very little focus, Antonio was close to getting kicked out of Roosevelt and never receiving his high school diploma. But in addition to his supportive mom, Antonio had a mentor at Roosevelt High who believed in him more than Antonio believed in himself. This was a guidance counselor named Herman Katz who loved the passion and the brilliant questions that spilled from this short, angry, troubled young man. Katz tried every way he could to convince Antonio to take the SAT and get back on a college-preparatory track.

Antonio wasn't budging. He was angry at his long-absent dad, angry at himself, and angry at life. So Katz decided to bend a rule and pay out of his own pocket for Antonio to take the test. That was a turning point. As Katz later recalled, "Antonio was bright, he was inquisitive. He just needed some direction." Antonio later commented, "Katz was an amazing teacher, counselor, human being. It makes a huge difference when you sense that someone is willing to go out of their way to believe in you and your future."

The unwavering support of this one stubborn mentor helped Antonio stay on track to finish his high school diploma at night school, then earn enough good grades at a community college to transfer eventually to the University of California at Los Angeles. At UCLA Antonio continued to develop strong friendships with other outsiders who were active in labor rights, who were leading the fight for better working conditions for thousands of grape workers, and who organized the demonstrations to end the war in Vietnam. Now, instead of always being viewed as a troublemaker or a "problem," Antonio was starting to acquire a reputation as a leader, a person whose enormous energy could get things done. After he graduated with a degree in history, he went on to law school.

Several years later, when Antonio married a strong and solid woman named Corina Raigosa, who was a Los Angeles school teacher, they wanted their new last name to reflect the equality of their relationship. So Villar and Raigosa became Villaraigosa (pronounced vee-yar-ray-go-sa). Together they built a family and Antonio Villaraigosa built a successful career as a union organizer. He quickly showed himself to be a dynamic speaker, an energetic problem-solver, and an incredible networker who built bridges connecting people of all backgrounds, faiths, and ethnicities. Soon he was offered an opportunity to work for a regional transportation agency that was trying to bring rapid transit back to Los Angeles. Then he was asked to run for the state legislature and represent his East Los Angeles neighborhood in Sacramento.

Because of his ability to cultivate friendships and alliances with so many diverse men and women in the state government, Villaraigosa eventually became the first Latino to be the Speaker of the California Assembly. Several years later, because of term limits, he had to give up his role as the leader of the state legislature. So he ran for mayor of Los Angeles in 2001, and he was close to victory until a very aggressive (and some have said racist) ad campaign that his opponent ran in the final week cost him the election.

Four years later, Villaraigosa ran once more against the same opponent. This time, with strong support from Latinos, Jews, African-Americans, liberal whites, younger voters, and even many moderate Republicans, Villaraigosa became the first Latino since 1872 to be elected mayor of the third largest city in the United States. Before long, he became a top advisor to the national leadership of the Democratic Party and many people were speculating that he might become the first Latino in modern times to be the governor of the nation's most populous state. Not bad for a kid who got booted out of high school.

Even though I've worked on two of his campaigns, I'm not saying that Antonio Villaraigosa is flawless or that I agree with every position he has taken as mayor. He still gets himself in trouble sometimes by his boldness, his impulsivity, and some highly publicized indiscretions in his personal life. My fourteen-year-old son, who has come with me to some of Villaraigosa's speeches, says bluntly, "He's way too hyper and he talks too loud."

But the high-energy young man from East Los Angeles who couldn't stop talking is still learning and growing. He has surrounded himself with a diverse group of intelligent men and women from all races, social classes, sexual orientations, and political beliefs. He seems to enjoy asking questions and listening to people who disagree with him on tough issues. He often explores the divergent opinions of environmentalists, feminists, bankers, union activists, and chamber of commerce executives before making up his own mind on important decisions. His enthusiasm, willingness to try new ideas, and ability to cultivate innovative alliances far exceed most other leaders. But none of these successes would have occurred if he hadn't been pushed by one particular mentor who refused to give up on him.

BEING A STUBBORN SUPPORTER

Have you ever seen a young person, a shunned outsider, losing faith in himself or herself, and yet sensed that this individual had gifts that needed to be shared with some corner of the world? Have you ever looked into someone's eyes, the way Herman Katz saw into young Antonio Villar, and realized, "This person has not been treated right yet. This person deserves more support than he or she has been getting"?

At a moment like that, your own rebellious side will serve you well. You may need to say to yourself, "This fragile and gifted individual is more important than whatever else I'm supposed to be doing today."

Then you may need to say directly to this person sitting in front of you, "I refuse to back down or give up on you. I will not turn my back on you even if you're starting to lose sight of your own gifts and purpose in life. You have something unique that deserves to be safeguarded and given support and time to flourish."

That's when your experiences as an outsider can come in handy, because you will then be taking your crucial place in an endless chain of quirky, original men and women who are sharing their strength and their courage with one another. Each of us heals our own pain from the past by opening up the future to someone else.

Chapter Ten

Making Your Circle the One People Want to Be In

This final chapter is about how to take the next step toward breaking out of isolation. In previous chapters we've explored the frustrations of being marginalized by groups that fail to appreciate who you are. Now it's time to focus on how to create genuinely positive group interactions in which you feel connected, strong, and fully at your best.

You won't be trying over and over again to fit in with what cliquish groups require (and often feeling like a fifth wheel). Instead, you will be offered several unusual but practical ideas for creating supportive connections with individuals who share your values. Rather than trying to squeeze yourself into a snobby circle of judgmental people where you probably won't feel comfortable, what if you were to establish your own circles—a few original, creative small group gatherings that are far more enjoyable and fulfilling?

I hope you're ready to try these ideas for yourself. They can lead to breakthroughs in every area of your life—work, family, volunteer groups, social events. All I ask is that you decide for yourself which of the following possibilities fit best for you or someone else in your life who has been an outsider.

Idea #1: A "Bring Your Own Favorite Music Night"

I often hear from clients, friends, and relatives that they long for a strong sense of community and connection, but find it very hard to come by in sprawling metropolitan areas where people tend to be so busy or live so far apart. Yet every once in a while, I learn about an innovative idea that's helped creative and original individuals to achieve a sense of exquisite connection—and have a good time while they're at it. The "Bring Your Own Favorite Music Night" is one such idea. Here's how it works:

Select a few creative or interesting people from work, from your personal life, or from a larger group where you have felt like an outsider and know the others have, too. Then invite several of them over to your place and ask them to bring one or two pieces of recorded music that have meaning for them. These might be classical pieces, recent pop songs, alternative music, or timeless standards—whatever has inspired them, comforted them, guided them, or even offended them.

Along with the music, invite each person to bring along some delicious food to share, plus a story—just a couple of minutes long—about why this particular song is important to his or her journey in life.

Don't worry about whether your living space is large or small, tidy or messy. All that matters is that you gather with a few creative, interesting individuals to share music and stories that will stir up ideas, feelings, and inspiration for each person present.

Twelve years ago my wife, Linda, and I tried this out. It was a genuine pleasure to have ten people from various parts of our lives settle into our cramped living room to share pieces of music that reflected some part of their journey. The stories behind the selections were interesting and revealing and helped us get to know one another on a deeper level. It proved to be an amazing evening.

A few years later I was counseling a sales rep named Leila who was recently divorced, feeling isolated, and having a hard time finding a sense of community in a large city. So I told her about the "Bring Your Own Favorite Music Night." She was reluctant at first. "What if the people from work and from my congregation find out that I live like a slob with cinder blocks and planks of wood for bookshelves?"

It took a few weeks for Leila to work through her insecure feelings and get up the courage to invite ten friends to her apartment for a music night. She sent out a flurry of e-mails and seven people said they would be there. On the night of the event, Leila was a bit disappointed when only four of the seven showed up.

But something wonderful happened at Leila's apartment that evening. She got to know these four people in a caring and profound way. Their musical choices and their personal stories, about how each specific song intersected with crucial moments and memories in their lives, were funny, tearful, entertaining, and deeply connecting.

One woman told an inspiring story about a beautiful song from her college days that always reminded her of her beloved husband, who had died suddenly three years earlier. A man had everyone laughing as he told about a provocative song from his early teenage years that used to drive his mother crazy, but that he loved to play at full blast from his messy bedroom. Another woman played a thought-provoking recent song that she'd happened to hear on the radio the day she decided to leave her abusive boyfriend and start a new life on her own.

Leila's party wasn't glamorous or flashy. But each person had a chance to be taken seriously and no one felt like an outsider. Before the magical night ended, the five of them decided to start meeting monthly and to invite one or two friends from each of their lives to join the group. The group grew to nine people, then twelve, then fourteen.

Now this monthly gathering that Leila launched is entering its fifth year. Everyone who takes part has told Leila in private how they've felt like unwelcome outsiders in other groups. Yet at the monthly "Bring Your Own Favorite Music" nights, every man and woman is on equal footing. They all have powerful memories of songs that have inspired them and comforted them. They all enjoy getting to know one another over pot-luck meals and rich stories of life and music.

Leila says, "It's one of the best ways I've ever seen to create a circle of friends who care about one another. Because we've shared deep stories each month about who we are and what we value most, several of us have started talking with one another on the phone and occasionally meeting for lunch as well. This huge city feels a lot less isolating and disconnected now."

Idea #2: Holiday Gatherings that Break the Rules

Every year at the holidays—Thanksgiving, Christmas, Hanukah, Kwanzaa, Easter, Passover, even the Fourth of July—many people feel isolated and discouraged because everyone else seems to have a place to go. But what if you have nowhere to spend the holiday that feels comfortable or welcoming? It might be because of a difficult or estranged family situation. Or it might be because you live far away from your family of origin and it's too expensive or exhausting to visit them for each major holiday. Or you might have a very different perspective than your other family members of what this holiday means and how you want to celebrate it.

To create a stronger sense of community and connection even if you are distant from your own relatives, you can put together an unconventional holiday gathering of your own. Here are some ways to do it:

- ✂ Invite several stranded souls to your place for a pot-luck meal where you all share stories about what you liked and disliked about the holidays while growing up.
- ✂ Go with several other outsiders—from work, from your neighborhood, or from other parts of your life—to a quiet restaurant where you can have a thoughtful conversation about the deeper meaning of the holiday.
- ✂ Ask a few people to join you for a movie, play, or other event that connects you with the underlying themes of the holiday. As you talk about it afterward, you can enjoy the chance to get to know the group on a deeper level.
- ✂ Create an Un-Holiday Celebration in which you invent rituals and start conversations quite different from the rituals of the mainstream holiday that no longer appeal to you.

One of my clients, a schoolteacher named Iris, found her distaste for the commercialization of Christmas growing over the years. So Iris and two of her more rebellious friends from work created an Un-Holiday Celebration each December. They make a conscious effort not to spend money on gifts. They use every dollar they save to create hand-decorated gift bags filled with food, clothes, and other useful treats for homeless people in their community.

Iris says, "I realize this might be offensive to some people, who insist that buying expensive gifts for hard-to-please family members is the true meaning of the holiday. But in recent years my two friends and I have enjoyed every moment of working together to create these gorgeous gift bags and to fill them with much-needed items. Then we spend a few hours on Christmas Day going around and giving the bags to homeless families in shelters and to solitary individuals whom we find in local parks and in doorways. We stay around for a while and talk about what's going on in their lives and what goals they have for the coming year. These have been the most meaningful holidays I can recall."

In your own life, is there some holiday that you would like to reconfigure in a way that rings true to your deepest values? Are there other rebellious individuals who might be willing to join you in putting new meaning and new compassion into holidays that have strayed from their original spiritual intentions? Or is there some other way you can make this holiday less about fitting in and more about what comes from your heart?

Idea #3: The Anti-Procrastination Partner

Let's explore another creative way to break out of isolation and build an important sense of connection in our hectic, fragmented lives. All of us have goals for our careers and our personal lives that sometimes get pushed aside by the pressures of daily living. You might dream of starting your own business or finishing a creative project that's been on hold. You might want to improve your health or change the way you deal with food and exercise. Or you might long to improve your love life or create more time to be with a family member or friend who needs you.

When any of these important goals get stalled or blocked, we have a choice. We can feel isolated and alone, without help from anyone. Or we can develop a creative and practical way to receive consistent support by identifying and cultivating a reliable anti-procrastination partner.

Try this for just one hour a week to stop being so isolated and to start creating the teamwork that will make you more effective on any important quest in your life:

- ⌘ Choose someone trustworthy in your life—a person of integrity from work, from one of your volunteer activities, from your high school or college days, or from a 12-step program or other support group. You may need to put two or three people on your list in case your first choice isn't interested in being an ongoing anti-procrastination partner.

- ⌘ Then call or write to this individual and explain how the two of you could collaborate one hour a week (or more, if you prefer) to tell each other your goals, dreams, and visions for the week, along with the specific steps you will take to meet those goals. This hour can be in person, over the phone, or even via e-mail or text message.

- ⌘ Each of you will take fifteen minutes to talk about what worked and what didn't work as you tried to meet last week's goals. Then take fifteen minutes to talk about your commitments and steps for the coming week.

- ⌘ The partner whose turn it is to listen is not to criticize, offer advice, or even make suggestions. All the listener has to do is be a sounding board and a genuine witness—a reliable presence who is caring and patient. The best results come from the simple act of declaring your goals, admitting your hesitations, and being accountable to someone who cares.

THE THERAPY CLIENT WHO DIDN'T WANT TO BE IN THERAPY

Let me tell you briefly about my client Ernesto, who used this anti-procrastination partner method in two areas of his life. Before he came to me for therapy, Ernesto had two goals that were constantly getting pushed aside by the demands of his high-pressure job.

The first goal was to deal with a prediabetic condition he'd been told could lead to full-blown diabetes unless he changed his diet and health habits. The second goal was to seek investors and partners for a terrific business idea that he had been too busy to pursue for several years.

Unfortunately, like many men, Ernesto tended to isolate himself and didn't like asking for help. In addition, Ernesto had grown up in a family where he felt like an outsider, and he'd learned to survive psychologically by keeping his goals and dreams secret from everyone else. Even though Ernesto kept promising himself that he was going to deal more effectively with his medical condition and to follow through on his excellent entrepreneurial idea, month after month he made very little progress on either goal. He was starting to get depressed and discouraged. On his last birthday, he'd said to himself, "I can see where this is going. I'm probably going to end up with serious health problems and stay stuck in the same dead-end job that I've wanted to leave for many years."

When his family doctor insisted that he needed to seek counseling to overcome his procrastination and distractibility, Ernesto called to make an appointment. But he told me clearly, "I don't want to get stuck in some long-term therapy. Can we make this quick?"

I offered him an incentive. "If you're willing to set up a once-a-week anti-procrastination partnership with someone you trust, I'll agree to let you stop coming to therapy sessions after only a few sessions."

Ernesto seemed pleasantly surprised that he was being given a chance to complete his counseling in just a few sessions, and he was motivated to make the therapy brief. So he called one of his best friends from college, who lived almost 2,000 miles away and had an unfulfilled business idea of his own. Together they set up a weekly cell-phone call in which each of them would spend fifteen minutes reviewing last week's goals and fifteen minutes declaring next week's goals and specific steps.

After just a few months in which we explored stress-reduction techniques and ways to stay on track with food and exercise goals, Ernesto came to my office and announced, "I've got good news, Doc. I'm eating better and I've cut back on sweets. I'm keeping my stress levels in check and I've started to exercise five times a week. Plus I'm talking each Sunday night to my anti-procrastination partner. And I've started to have productive meetings a few times a week to find investors for my business idea. I'm finally back on track, and a lot of the progress is because I absolutely don't want to let my old friend from college see me fail at this. Like you said, Doc, I just needed to be accountable to someone and to know I'm being watched carefully by a person I respect who's rooting for me to succeed at these goals. Do you think I'm ready to take a break from therapy for a while?"

While some people make quick progress like this, many others are much slower to realize changes. I did think Ernesto was ready, so I smiled at him and said, "Good work. Just call me every two weeks and let me know if you need a tune-up every so often." Since then he's called twice a month for a quick ten-minute phone check-in, and he's also come into my office for one-on-one problem-solving on three occasions. I have great respect for a person who's willing to work hard and keep his promises in order to avoid being in permanent therapy.

Like Ernesto, many of us have enormously busy schedules that can derail our deepest desires for our lives. If there are goals in your own life that you've put on hold and you're feeling isolated or discouraged, I urge you to give yourself the possibility of a breakthrough by connecting with a weekly anti-procrastination partner.

It doesn't have to be someone who's flawless. It doesn't even have to be someone who's nearby. It just has to be someone whom you trust, who can check in weekly via phone or e-mail without giving unsolicited advice, and who cares enough to want both of you to succeed at your most cherished goals. Certainly there is at least one person you can think of who fits that description and who would be willing to spend just one hour a week making sure the two of you bring to fruition the dreams and visions you have been putting off for too long.

Idea #4: Becoming a Change-Maker Who Creates New Circles

Before we end this chapter and this book, there's one more break from tradition that I want you to consider for moving out of isolation. This final method is especially useful when you're trying to do good in the world but you're feeling alone or unsupported in your efforts.

When you think of someone who is standing up for an important cause or battling the status quo, you probably envision a lonely, isolated individual who's up against insurmountable odds. In films and novels, the person trying to make important change is a loner like Norma Rae (the role that won an Academy Award for Sally Field), speaking up for the union in a town that doesn't like unions. Or an outsider like Atticus Finch in Harper Lee's *To Kill a Mockingbird* (played by Gregory Peck in the film), defending an innocent man in a town that has already convicted him in its own mind. This is a classic theme of great drama: the passionate loner who has to work in painful isolation.

But fortunately, there's a less dramatic and far more balanced way to stand up for something you believe in. Many change-makers in this world do it differently from the lonely heroes of classic books and films. Rather than assuming that no one is on their side, these people envision and help to create a growing circle of supportive individuals who are willing to share the toughest tasks of important projects. In fact, research shows that the most successful change-makers in all areas of society tend to be those who join with other open-minded people to build a sense of community and teamwork even as they are making much-needed repairs to this broken world.

Think about something large or small you want to change in your corner of the planet. Then imagine having several dedicated, creative, and caring people on your side as you seek ways to improve the situation. Envision what it would be like if you were at the center of a circle of decent and thoughtful people who could share the hard work and offer terrific ideas on how to address something that you each knew in your heart needed to be addressed.

Surrounding yourself with people who support your vision is not as hard as you might think it is. It might be a small team you are building to address a troublesome issue in your family, your school, your workplace, or your community that you've tried to improve on your own (but had your efforts frustrated). But what if you empower even a small group of caring people who share your concerns and who want to add their insights and connections to your efforts for making important changes? What if you stop thinking of yourself as a lone wolf and start to think of yourself as part of a new kind of group that's focused on healing something that desperately needs to be healed?

A friend and colleague I've known for twenty-five years has taught me how crucial it is to have teammates when you're trying to shake things up in a positive way. I hope his story sparks ideas for how to break out of isolation and create support for your own passionate quest.

THE SOFT-SPOKEN KID WITH "CRAZY" IDEAS

My friend Andy Lipkis has always looked like a down-to-earth, regular guy. But underneath his casual clothes and his soft-spoken demeanor, Andy has never thought like the majority.

When Andy was fifteen, an age when most boys were focused on sports, science fiction, or girls, Andy was worried about trees. He had heard that the smog in major cities was killing the forests and that entire species of trees were becoming extinct. A sensitive soul, Andy was upset and determined to do something about it.

At a summer camp in the San Bernardino Mountains thirty miles east of Los Angeles, where the counselors often talked about the importance of repairing the world, this isolated fifteen-year-old got the beginnings of an unusual (some adults said "crazy") idea. He had done some research and figured out that even though thousands of trees were dying each year, certain species of trees were smog-resistant and could significantly improve the air quality if planted in large enough numbers. He decided that he wanted to build a summer camp that would be focused on kids planting trees and taking care of them in order to reduce overall smog levels. But the idea was too costly and he couldn't find a way to make it happen.

So Andy came up with a Plan B: he would arrange for smog-resistant trees to be supplied free of charge to existing summer camps for kids to plant. He realized he wasn't going to be able to do this alone. In order to make even the smallest impact on urban pollution, he would need to find a way to arrange for many thousands of smog-resistant trees to be distributed, planted, and cared for until they were large and strong enough to grow on their own. Then he got the idea to work during the spring months with urban public schools and retirement homes where volunteers would help pot the trees in cartons so that they could be planted each summer by kids at camps in the forests and mountains nearby. But before he got too far with this idea, he found out the logistics proved very costly and hard to implement.

Even while he was finishing high school and trying to act like a normal teenager, Andy kept worrying that trees were dying and the air was suffering much more than just a few thousand smog-resistant trees could remedy. So he kept looking for opportunities to make a larger difference. He found out that 20,000 smog-resistant redwoods and pines growing in a Department of Forestry nursery might be available for planting if there were enough volunteers. But the department policy required that these trees be purchased rather than donated, so Andy—by then a nineteen-year-old college freshman—would have to come up with $600, which he simply didn't have.

Instead, Andy came up with another wild idea. He talked someone at the *Los Angeles Times* into running an article about the need to plant smog-resistant trees and the fact that if students donated fifty cents or a dollar of their spare change, it could be done. Within a few weeks, the response to the article brought in over $10,000 in donations. The 20,000 smog-resistant redwoods and pines were purchased and planted. To manage the money properly, Andy formed a nonprofit organization called TreePeople.

From then on, TreePeople followed this same essential model: empowering lots of compassionate people to plant large numbers of trees that could begin to restore the ecological balance in urban communities. Even though he was still a soft-spoken, down-to-earth, regular guy, Andy kept telling his story to groups of people, moving many in each audience to join in and offer their support.

At first many public officials, scientists, and ecology scholars were skeptical about TreePeople. Yet each time Andy described his vision to another group of people and showed them what might happen if enough people felt responsibility for the trees and the air where they lived or went to school, more and more volunteers signed up. And not as passive donors or one-time supporters. TreePeople works by organizing people of all ages—one school classroom at a time, one retirement home at a time, one city block at a time, one church, mosque, or temple youth group at a time—to reclaim their neighborhoods by planting trees and then *caring* for those trees. Since a new tree needs care for five years before it's strong enough to survive on its own, this is a community commitment that keeps people involved.

It's quite something to watch the diverse residents of tough, middle-income, or affluent neighborhoods come forward to plant, care for, and watch over their very own trees. Even kids and adults who have felt isolated or powerless in life seem to come alive when they talk about their trees and how they're taking care of these living beings as long as they're needed.

CREATING A SUSTAINABLE CIRCLE OF SUPPORT

It's normal to be a bit skeptical and ask just how much one person can accomplish by creating a circle of people who share his or her values. In Andy's case, the original training materials and volunteer team-building sessions that he put together eventually sparked over 90,000 elementary school kids per year to enhance the beauty and improve the air quality around their homes and schools. In addition, several hundred thousand people of all ages—from teens to senior citizens—have been trained by TreePeople volunteers and staff to get together in small groups of Citizen Foresters and take care of several trees per person to change the face of the urban sprawl.

By creating numerous intimate circles of people who want to live in a healthier environment, TreePeople successfully facilitated the planting of several million new trees in the Los Angeles area. They also organized neighborhoods and schools to respond quickly to natural disasters as trained emergency teams, piling up sandbags whenever there is flooding in the narrow canyons or cutting down brush when there are fires due to drought conditions and strong winds. Talking to one small group at a time, Andy and his staff have gradually convinced millions of urban men and women to plant and care for shade trees alongside their homes, which can dramatically reduce energy costs and the demand for fossil fuels.

TreePeople has also worked with hundreds of urban schools to tear up their heat-trapping asphalt playgrounds and replace them with gardens, comfortable shady places to sit, and more user-friendly play areas. At first no one believed that school district officials would be willing to invest the time and money to dig up the flat black-tar playgrounds that were a fixture at all the elementary, junior high, and high schools. But when TreePeople showed them how much money they would save in energy costs from replacing these hot, sticky surfaces with shade trees and greener materials, the school districts began to sign up for change.

In addition, Andy and TreePeople were among the first to speak up and educate skeptical city-dwellers about what was then a radical new concept called recycling. They worked for many years to teach politicians and community leaders the benefits of giving free recycling bins to homeowners throughout the metropolitan area and the huge profits that could be generated from recycled cardboard, newspapers, glass, plastics, and yard waste. At first, opponents claimed that people were too selfish to change old habits, but now there are over five million people in Southern California who recycle weekly as a result of the programs that Andy and his circle explained to one politician and community group at a time.

All his adult life, Andy has been offered lucrative chances to leave TreePeople to work as a nonprofit executive in some other city or country. But he's chosen each time to stay close to home, build a loving family with his wife, Katie, and their two children, and keep TreePeople a sane and healthy place to be an employee or a volunteer. He's continually coming up with "crazy" new ideas to expand the reach of the circle he created back when he was an idealistic teenager who realized he couldn't do it all alone. The latest involves teaching community leaders and real-estate developers how to build experimental houses and neighborhoods that store and reuse the rainfall that comes only a few months each year to Southwestern cities. To prove it was workable, Andy retrofitted a 1920s bungalow to demonstrate how special drains, downspouts, and cisterns could successfully reuse the rainwater and lessen water consumption costs. The retrofitted house also has a heat-reflecting roof and strategically placed trees that cool it and reduce air conditioning costs.

Andy's idea will eventually save homeowners and cities millions of dollars. Several neighborhoods have signed up to have their homes retrofitted according to Andy's new approach. And it's helping people envision new possibilities for drought prevention in other United States cities and around the world.

If you met Andy today on the street, you would see he's still a down-to-earth guy who just happens to be the soft-spoken center of thousands of small circles in which passionate men and women join together to beautify their urban neighborhoods, take care of a few trees per person, and create lasting change. You'd never know he'd received awards from the United Nations, the International Olympic Committee, or various environmental organizations. You'd just know you were talking with a caring, humble man who wanted to tell you his story.

WHOM WILL YOU INVITE INTO YOUR NEW CIRCLE?

As you think about your own life and the changes you want to see in your family, your workplace, your volunteer groups, your social circles, or your neighborhood, town, or city, stop and ask yourself, "Have I been too much of a lone wolf? Is there someone who might share my ideas and be willing to join a change-makers' team? Is there a way to get others involved and make these changes more feasible?"

As Andy Lipkis has shown, coming up with a realistic plan for genuine teamwork is essential. It starts with a simple first step—identifying just a few people who share your values and can brainstorm with you on how to make changes happen.

But in order to start that first brainstorming conversation, you'll need to imagine yourself as the hub of a new circle rather than a shunned outsider in some old one. If you've felt like an outsider for a long time, this shift may seem unfamiliar or uncomfortable at first. But I hope that you can begin to imagine it. Then I hope you can identify a few supportive people who might want to join you in improving some aspect of life that you care about deeply. All it takes is a few phone calls to get things rolling.

You might be amazed at how many people share your point of view but have been waiting for someone like you to get things started. Please don't hold your breath and wait for someone else to make the first move. Use your passion and your own "crazy" ideas to build a circle of your own.

One More Shift from Isolation to New Circles of Compassion

I want to tell you one last story about an unwelcome outsider who turned isolation into connection. This woman was born out of wedlock in a small, poor town in Mississippi. When her troubled mother left Mississippi to move to Milwaukee and look for work, the girl lived for several years with her grandmother and helped her raise pigs and chickens on their tiny plot of land. She felt unattractive and different from her peers, she was told over and over that she didn't fit in, and she spent much of her childhood looking at the world through the eyes of an outsider because of factors beyond her control. Her name is Oprah Winfrey.

When you think about this charismatic and powerful woman, you probably can't imagine her as a self-doubting young girl who wished she could fit in and spent most of her time alone. But over the years, Oprah has revealed a great deal about her early life as a child living in poverty in the South. She admits, "I was raised with an outhouse, no plumbing. Nobody had any clue that my life could be anything but working in some factory or a cotton field in Mississippi."

Oprah was close to her grandma, who taught her to love reading books. But she lived in fear of her grandfather, whom she describes as "always a dark presence. I remember him always throwing things at me or trying to shoo me away with his cane." Then, when she was six, Oprah moved to Milwaukee to live with her mother, who during those years had two more children and no husband and worked long hours cleaning houses. "My mother was often tired or angry and hostile," Oprah remembers. "I told the biggest lies in school about my family because I wanted to be like everybody else."

Her mother deeply resented Oprah's love of books and her constant desire to learn about the outside world through reading. Oprah explains, "Not only was my mother not a reader, but I remember being in the back hallway when I was about nine—I'm going to try to say this without crying—and my mother threw the door open and grabbed a book out of my hand and said, 'You're nothing but a something-something bookworm. Get your butt outside!' I was treated as though something was wrong with me because I wanted to read all the time."

Because her mom was at work on most days, Oprah was frequently cared for by a nineteen-year-old cousin. But when Oprah was nine, he molested her and then made her promise never to tell. It was a secret she kept to herself for many years, until a guest on *The Oprah Winfrey Show* talked about her own memories of being molested at a young age. Oprah then spoke for the first time about the sense of isolation she had lived with for so many years because she never felt it was safe to tell anyone about her own experiences.

After constantly clashing with her mother in Milwaukee, Oprah moved to Nashville to try living with her father, which was a little better at first. But then at age thirteen she was molested by another male relative. She later described the pain and aloneness she felt as a teenager when she used sex to try to please older boys and men who didn't really respect her. She says, "I was one of the girls who was abused because I couldn't say no, because it was more important for me to please the abuser than to please myself. I didn't want the boys to be mad at me. You know what my biggest fault is? I don't have the courage to be disliked."

Though she was a bright student, she felt isolated in school because the other kids resented her for it. She explains, "If you grow up a bully and that works, that's what you do. If you're the class clown and that works, that's what you do. I was always the smartest kid in class and that worked for me—by third grade I had it figured out. So I was the one who would read the assignment early and turn the paper in ahead of time. That makes everyone else hate you, but that's what worked for me."

But during her high school years she began to reach out and get involved in after-school community service activities, fundraisers, and church programs. During one of her fundraising projects, she asked a local Nashville radio station for a donation. There she impressed the disc jockey so much with her poise and speaking voice that he agreed to let her do her first demo tape, which got her a part-time job in radio, reading the evening news for $100 a week.

Once Oprah discovered her gift for talking comfortably into a microphone, her life began to change. At age nineteen she became the first woman and the first African-American to anchor the news at a Nashville television station. Then she became a media star in Baltimore, anchoring the 6 o'clock news. But her producers felt she was too emotional when reading the news copy, so she was demoted to a morning show called *People Are Talking*, where she was supposed to deal with current topics that were considered less "hard news."

According to Oprah, "The minute the first show was over, I thought, 'Thank God, I've found what I was meant to do.' It's like breathing to me." Over the next few years she built *People Are Talking* into a highly-rated program that explored the most pressing personal and social issues of the day.

Then a few years later she moved to Chicago to host the popular *AM Chicago* program, where she was so compelling as a host the show was soon renamed *The Oprah Winfrey Show*. As you probably know, it became one of the highest-rated programs ever on television and a place where millions of people tuned-in daily to explore highly personal topics that no one else had the guts to discuss.

It also became the vehicle that allowed Oprah to reach out to children who were going through what she had. She launched a national campaign to educate people to prevent child abuse and to create an extensive data bank of convicted offenders of abuse and other serious crimes. She opened a Boys and Girls Club in her hometown of Kosciusko, Mississippi, to help kids have fun at supervised after-school activities and to build positive friendships.

A CIRCLE OF PASSION AND IDEAS

Several years ago, I met Oprah for the first time when I was invited to talk about one of my books on her program. When I was backstage before the show, even though I was nervous, I saw a few things that I will never forget.

First, I discovered that this charismatic woman whom I had watched on television many times was part of an amazing team of co-producers and staff who were so comfortable with each other and their boss that they could brainstorm, argue, offer alternatives, and come to decisions without holding anything back. I watched two intense conversations in which Oprah took her place as part of a lively circle of intelligent colleagues who weren't afraid to challenge her as they worked to come up with creative solutions to intense issues that needed to get resolved quickly because the cameras were going to roll in just a few minutes.

I've worked in large and small companies and been part of many nonprofit organizations. But I've rarely seen a staff meeting so passionate and uninhibited, where everyone seemed to feel so comfortable disagreeing with one another openly and working quickly toward a healthy consensus on complicated decisions.

On that visit, in the hallway outside the green room, I also happened to hear a beautiful conversation between Oprah and her friend Gayle King, a Hartford, Connecticut, talk-show host who has been Oprah's confidante for many years. Gayle King was in Chicago on that particular Tuesday, visiting backstage, and the two women were laughing, telling stories, and catching up on life just minutes before filming began.

I have seen many celebrities try to let their hair down, but the majority of them aren't able to be fully relaxed, authentic or unguarded when they're off camera. Yet watching Oprah and her friend Gayle in their free-flowing conversation, I had the sense that these two women had developed an exquisite trust and sense of safety with one another.

"In spite of all the things that have happened to me," Oprah has said of her thirty-year friendship with Gayle King, "we laugh every night about one thing or another. She absolutely keeps me grounded."

Creating Your Own Trusted Circles

Seeing up close how comfortably Oprah is able to work with strong-minded teammates and to maintain a close, enduring friendship in ways she probably couldn't do when she was an isolated child, I wondered if that's what most of us are trying to do in our adult lives. We may have felt alone or disconnected at times in our early, awkward years, but as adults we have more perspective and greater capacities from which to create lasting friendships, strong teamwork, and positive alliances.

Yet these connections don't just happen without some effort and commitment. Nor can we sit back and simply wait for someone else to make the effort—to initiate the conversations that will move these relationships forward.

What about your own life? Is there someone at work or in your neighborhood whom you value as a friend but don't find the time to keep reaching out to and create a stronger bond? If so, I hope this advice on strengthening your circles of connection will spark you to reach out with e-mail or a phone call.

Or is there someone in your past, someone you care about from high school, college, or another important time in your life, with whom you have a strong unspoken connection that you've let drift away? If so, I hope you will seize this opportunity to make contact with this person and see if the two of you can still be there for each other.

Or, as you work on the issues and projects that you care about deeply, is there someone doing similar work whom you admire but feel too shy to contact directly? Now might be the time to reach out to this person, let him or her know your interest, and ask how you can support each other's efforts. Someone you thought wouldn't give you the time of day may respond to a heartfelt letter, e-mail, or phone call if the two of you share some common goal or experience.

In this chapter and throughout this book, we've explored how, once you begin to appreciate who you are and reach out to others who are capable of understanding your ideas, your world starts to expand. The fact that you were shunned or criticized long ago, just for being a remarkably original human being, doesn't mean that your adult life has to be constricted. In my experience, the people who were outside the mainstream early in life often turn out to be the boldest and most valuable trailblazers.

The key is to stop pretending you are anyone other than who you are and to start honoring the unique perspective you've been given—by God, genetics, or your life experiences—to share with the world. I thank you for reading whatever sections of this book you've read, and I applaud you for your willingness to take the risk of becoming a more authentic human being. As you continue on your journey in life, I hope you will connect with allies, teammates, and friends who will make your journey a lot less lonely and far more enjoyable.

Sources, Notes, and Recommended Readings

Chapter Two

Page 16: The comments and facts about Dr. Viktor Frankl are from personal conversations in 1979 and 1988 with the author, as well as from Viktor Frankl, *Man's Search for Meaning*, New York: Pocket Books, 1985, and *The Doctor and the Soul*, New York: Vintage, 1986.

Page 18: "Research shows that the need for connection and for a place to belong is a basic trait in most mammals and especially humans…" can be found in Reg Williams, Bonnie Hagerty, and Chanokruthai Choenarom, *Archives of Psychiatric Nursing*, April 2005; Petra Bohnke, "First European Quality of Life Survey," Berlin, Germany: Social Science Research Centre, 2005; and Matthew Capps, *Journal of Educational Research and Social Policy*, vol. 4:2, pages 1–20, Fall 2004.

Page 19: "Mammals and humans are hard-wired to release adrenalin when left out or excluded…" can be found in Walter Cannon, *American Journal of Psychology*, vol. 39, pages 106–124, 1927, and Daniel J. Siegel, *The Developing Mind*, New York: Guilford, 2001.

Page 24: "Discovering how to find allies and teammates for raising kids with special needs…" can be found in "Success stories of parents with special needs children" at www.specialchild.com, and in "Support groups and information links for parents helping parents" at www.php.com.

Chapter Three

Page 26: The details and quotes regarding Bettye Goldstein (Betty Friedan) are from: personal conversations between Ms. Friedan and the author during the 1980s in Los Angeles, as well by Betty Friedan, *Life So Far: A Memoir*, New York: Simon & Schuster, 2000; *The Feminine Mystique*, revised edition, New York: Norton, 2001; Milton Meltzer, *Betty Friedan: A Voice for Women's Rights*, New York: Puffin, 1986; and Lisa Frederiksen Bohannon, *Women's*

Work: The Story of Betty Friedan, Greensboro, North Carolina: Morgan Reynolds Books, 2004.

Page 31: The description of Charles Schwab is from Betsy Morris, "Ovecoming Dyslexia," *Fortune,* vol. 145:10, pages 54–59 and Christina Cheakalos, Bruce Frankel, William Plummer, and Susan Schindehette, "Heavy Mettle: Overcoming Learning Disabilities," *People Weekly,* 54: 18, October 30, 2000, pages 56–58.

Page 31: The comments about Paul Orfalea, founder of Kinkos, are from Paul Orfalea and Ann Marsh, *Copy This!: Lessons from a Hyperactive Dyslexic,* New York: Workman, 2005.

Page 31: The information about John Chambers of Cisco is from Betsy Morris, "Overcoming Dyslexia," *Fortune,* 145:10, pages 54–59.

Page 31: The comments about Mrs. Fields are from Debbi Fields and Alan Furst, *One Smart Cookie,* New York: Simon and Schuster, 1987.

Page 32–33: The details about explorer, scientist and teacher Ann Bancroft are from Liv Arnesen and Ann Bancroft, *No Horizon Is So Far,* New York: Penguin, 2003.

Page 35: For more information about books on how to refocus each day and deal effectively with distractibility, see Edward Hallowell and John Ratey, *Delivered from Distraction: Getting the Most Out of Life with Attention Deficit Disorder,* New York: Ballantine, 2005; Kate Kelly and Peggy Ramundo, *You Mean I'm Not Lazy, Crazy or Stupid,* New York: Scribner, 1995; and Judith Kolberg, *ADD-Friendly Ways to Organize Your Life,* New York: Routledge, 2002.

Page 39: The information about Alex Haley is from personal conversations between Haley and the author in 1976–1978 at Doubleday offices in New York; "Alex Haley," *Contemporary Black Biography,* Farmington Hills,

Writing Career," *Writer's Digest,* vol. 60, August 1980, p. 20; and Betty Winston Baye, "Alex Haley's Roots Revisited," *Essence Magazine,* February 1992, p. 88.

Page 43: The book by Hope Edelman is *Motherless Daughters: The Legacy of Loss,* New York: Da Capo Press, 1994.

Page 45: The details and quotes regarding Ang Lee are from three individuals who have worked closely with him, as well as Michelle Kung, "Ang Lee's Long Climb to Brokeback Mountain," *Entertainment Weekly,* December 12, 2005, p. 40; "Ang Lee," *Biography Resource Center,* Farmington Hills, Michigan.: Gale Research, 2006; Ann Hornaday, "A Director's Trip," *New York Times,* August 1, 1993, sec. 2, p. 25; Min Lee, "Lee Disappointed Over Brokeback Loss," Associated Press/Yahoo News, March 8, 2006; and "The Directors Roundtable," *Newsweek,* February 6, 2006, p. 66.

Chapter Four

Page 52: "Memories of being an outsider lodge in a few particular cells..." is described in J. Douglas Bremner, *Does Stress Damage the Brain,* New York: Norton, 2005; Daniel J. Siegel, *The Developing Mind,* New York: Guilford, 2001; and Bessel Van der Kolk, Alexander McFarlane and Lars Weisaeth, *Traumatic Stress,* New York: Guilford, 2006.

Page 59: "From the perspective of brain biochemistry, these two opposing visualization questions have a remarkable ability to deactivate the anxious and angry part of the brain..." is described in Daniel J. Siegel, *The Mindful Brain,* New York: Norton, 2007.

Page 61: The story of Rabbi Zusya of Hanipol comes from numerous sources including Martin Buber, *Tales of Hasidim: Early Masters,* New York: Schocken Books, 1947.

Page 64: "Little Miss Sunshine" was written by Michael Arndt, directed by Jonathan Dayton and Valerie Faris, and produced by Big Beach Films.

Page 64: "'Little Miss Sunshine' hilariously punctures the grotesque bubble" was written by Carina Chocano, "The Sun Doesn't Shine on Delusion," *Los Angeles Times,* July 26, 2006, page E:1.

Page 71: For more on the research about insecurities or perfectionism for adoptees, see Marlou Russell, *Adoption Wisdom: A Guide to the Issues and Feelings of Adoption,* California: Broken Branch, 1996; and David Brodzinsky, Marshall Schechter, and Robin Marantz Henig, *Being Adopted: The Lifelong Search for Self,* New York: Anchor, 1993.

Page 72: The comments and quotes regarding Faith Hill are from Kate Coyne, "Faith Hill Fesses Up," *Good Housekeeping,* April 2002, 234:4, p. 94; Jeanne Wolf, "Keeping the Faith," *Redbook,* June 2000, 194:6, p. 118; and Peg Rosen, "Give Faith a Break," *Redbook,* December 2001, 197:6, p. 80.

Page 74: The spiritual method of being both a grain of sand and a unique, amazing individual comes from ancient and modern Jewish Hasidic teachings that combine Genesis 18:27 (in which Abraham says we are all "dust and ashes") with the Talmudic discussion in Sanhedrin 37a (that suggests "every person is obliged to say the world was created for my sake—that I am here for the chance to do a good deed that can illuminate darkness with holiness and light").

Chapter Five

Page 79: For more information about staying professional and having effective comeback lines when you're dealing with emotionally abusive people at work, see Leonard Felder, *Does Someone at Work Treat You Badly,* New York: Berkley Books, 1993.

Chapter Six

Page 98: For the economists' viewpoints on competing for precious commodities, see Stephen Happel, *Economics: An Examination of Scarcity*, New Jersey: Thomas Horton and Daughters Press, 2000.

Page 99: For the psychologists' viewpoints on the origins of cliques as a chance to defend oneself against inner discomfort by making someone else uncomfortable instead, see M. Brewer, "In-Group Bias," *Psychological Bulletin*, 86:307–324; and J.M. Rabbie, "The Effects of Intergroup Competition-Cooperation on Intra- and Intergroup Relationships," in J. Grzelak and V. Derlega, *Living with Other People*, New York: Academic Press, 1981.

Page 99: For psychological experiments in which normally well-mannered and decent people acted in a mean way to put down someone else, see W.G. Austin and S. Worchel, *The Social Psychology of Intergroup Relationships*, California: Brooks-Cole, 1979; Muzafer Sherif, *Intergroup Conflict and Cooperation*, Oklahoma: The University of Oklahoma Press, 1961; and Philip Zimbardo, *The Lucifer Effect*, New York: Random House, 2007.

Page 106: "Apocalypse Now" was written by John Milius and Francis Ford Coppola, directed by Francis Ford Coppola, and produced by Zoetrope Studios. The character referred to is Lieutenant Colonel Bill Kilgore, played by Robert Duvall.

Chapter Seven

Page 113: For more about improving difficult family relationships, see Leonard Felder, *When Difficult Relatives Happen to Good People*, Pennsylvania: Rodale, 2003.

Chapter Eight

Page 139: Facts about the astronomer Galileo come from James Reston, *Galileo: A Life*, Frederick, Maryland.: Beard Books, 2000; Peter Machamer, *The Cambridge Companion to Galileo*, London: Cambridge University Press,

Cambridge Companion to Galileo, London: Cambridge University Press, 1998; and Jerome Langford, *Galileo, Science, and the Church*, Indiana: St. Augustine Press, 1998.

Page 149: The facts about Henry Thoreau's book sales are from Walter Harding, *The Days of Henry Thoreau*, New York: Knopf, 1965, p. 340; and Joseph Wood Krutch, *Henry David Thoreau*, New York: William Sloane Associates, 1948, p. 103.

Page 150: The quotes and details about Natalie McIntyre (Macy Gray) are from conversations with students and parents from the Macy Gray Music Academy; Alison Powell, "Gray's Day," *Interview*, 30: 3 (March 2000), p. 66; Rob Bruner, "There's Something About Macy," *Entertainment Weekly*, 496 (July 30, 1999), p. 72; Veronica Chambers, "Macy Gray Makes a Scene," *Newsweek*, 134: 5 (August 2, 1999), p. 62; Steve Dougherty, "Shades of Gray," *People Weekly*, Vol. 55: 10 (March 12, 2001), p. 91–92; Ed Leibowitz, "In a Major Key," *Los Angeles Magazine*, 51:8 (August 2006), p. 50; and Joan Morgan, "The Trouble with Being Macy," *Essence*, 34: 9 (January 2004), p. 100.

Chapter Nine

Page 158: For research about what helps psychological resilience, see Bonnie Benard, *Resiliency: What We Have Learned*, San Francisco: West Ed, 2004; Karen Reivich and Andrew Shatte, *The Resilience Factor*, New York: Broadway Books, 2002; and Michael Resnick, "Protective Factors, Resiliency, and Healthy Youth Development," *Adolescent Medicine: State of the Art Reviews*, 11: 1, February, p. 157–164.

Page 160: The statement about Desmond Tutu and the compassionate priest is from two sources: a speech that Archbishop Tutu gave in Los Angeles in the mid-1980s and Martin Copenhaver, *To Begin at the Beginning*, Cleveland: United Church Press, 1994, p. 248.

Page 168: The facts and quotes regarding Yo-Yo Ma are from "Yo-Yo Ma, *Encyclopedia of World Biography*, Vol. 20, Farmington Hills, Michigan.: Gale

Group, 2000; "Yo-Yo Ma," *Notable Asian Americans*, Farmington Hills, Michigan: Gale Research, 1995; Matthew Gurewitsch, "Master Ma," *Town and Country*, 152: 5213, February 1998, p. 47; Alex Ross, "Journey's End: Yo-Yo Ma's Asian Trek," *The New Yorker*, 78:13, May 27, 2002, p. 122; and Susan Jakes, "Yo-Yo Ma: Taking Flight on a Musical Journey Without Borders," *Time International*, Vol. 161:16, April 28, 2003, p. 38.

Page 173: For more on how to open up to new ideas for new paradigms after years of thinking a certain way, see Thomas S. Kuhn, *The Structure of Scientific Revolutions*, Chicago: University of Chicago Press, 1962.

Page173: The details and quotes regarding Dr. Elisabeth Kübler-Ross are from personal conversations in 1978–1979 with the author; Elisabeth Kübler-Ross, *The Wheel of Life: A Memoir of Living and Dying*, New York: Scribner, 1997; Derek Gill, *Quest: The Life of Elisabeth Kübler-Ross*, New York: Harper, 1980; and "Elisabeth Kübler-Ross," *American Decades*, Farmington Hills, Michigan: Gale Research, 1998.

Page 179: The facts and quotes about Antonio Villaraigosa and Herman Katz are from personal conversations with several associates of the mayor; Robin Abcarian, "Spotlight on a Longtime Villaraigosa Supporter," *Los Angeles Times*, July 2, 2005, p. E-1; Tina Daunt, "Early Challenges, Different Paths, Same Goal," *Los Angeles Times*, May 8, 2005, p. A:1; Matea Gold, "His Second Chance Shaped Villaraigosa," *Los Angeles Times*, May 31, 2001, p. B-1; Hector Tobar, "Profile: Antonio Villaraigosa," *Los Angeles Times*, March 16, 2001, p. A-1; Andrew Murr, "The Survivor's Story," *Newsweek*, May 30, 2005, p. 32; and Deborah White, "The Bumpy Road of a Rising Democratic Superstar," *About.com (About: Liberal Politics)*.

Chapter Ten
Page 191: "Norma Rae" was written by Harriet Frank, Jr. and Martin Ravitch, directed by Martin Ritt, and distributed by Twentieth Century Fox.

Page 191: The 1962 film "To Kill a Mockingbird" was written by Harper Lee and Horton Foote, directed by Robert Mulligan, and produced by Brentwood Productions.

Page 192: The details and quotes regarding Andy Lipkis are from personal conversations with the author, 1983-2007, as well as Andy Lipkis, *The Simple Act of Planting a Tree,* Los Angeles, Tarcher, 1990; Judith Lewis, "Citizen Forester," *LA Weekly,* April 14, 2005; Jennifer Price, "Like Water for Concrete: From Flood Control to Watershed Management," *LA Weekly,* August 8, 2001; "Andy Lipkis," *Contemporary Newsmakers,* Farmington Hills, Michigan: Gale Research, 2007; Joseph Anthony, "Roots: Treepeople Plants Trees," *Mother Jones,* 15: 36, April-May 1990, p. 18; Janice Simpson, "For Goodness' Sake," *Time,* 133:2, January 13, 1989, p. 20; Virginia Morell, "Planting Awareness with the Tree People," *American Forests,* Vol 87, November 1981, p. 22; and Tracy Rysavy, "Treepeople," *Yes!Magazine,* Bainbridge Island, Washington.: Positive Futures Network, Winter 2000.

Page 197: The details and quotes about Oprah Winfrey are from personal conversations between the author and various staff on the Oprah Winfrey Show, April 1989; Belinda Friedrich, *Oprah Winfrey,* Philadelphia: Chelsea House, 2001; Janet Lowe, *Oprah Speaks,* New York: John Wiley, 1998; Robert Waldron, *Oprah!,* New York: St. Martins Press, 1987; Chris Anderson, "Meet Oprah Winfrey," *Good Housekeeping,* August 1986, p. 32; Judy Markey, "Brassy, Sassy Oprah Winfrey," *Cosmopolitan,* September 1986, p. 99; Marcia Ann Gillespie, "Winfrey Takes All," *Ms. Magazine,* November 1988, p. 54; Marjorie Rosen, "Oprah Overcomes," *People Weekly,* January 10, 1994, p. 42; Jill Brooke Coiner, "Oprah Sets Record Straight," *McCall's,* November 1993, p. 149; "Seven Stars Say What Makes a Good Friend," *Redbook,* October 1989, p. 22; "Gayle King Makes Talk Show History," *Jet,* October 22, 1997, p. 54; "Oprah Winfrey: A Life in Books," *Life Magazine,* September 1997, p. 9; and Judy Markey, "Opinionated Oprah," *Woman's Day,* October 4, 1988, p. 71.

Index

About the Author

Leonard Felder, Ph.D., is a licensed psychologist in private practice. He has written ten books that have sold more than one million copies and have been translated into fourteen languages. His titles include *When Difficult Relatives Happen to Good People, The Ten Challenges, Seven Prayers That Can Change Your Life, Does Someone at Work Treat You Badly?, Wake Up or Break Up, Making Peace with Your Parents,* and *Making Peace with Yourself.*

Dr. Felder has appeared on over two hundred radio and television programs, including *The Oprah Winfrey Show,* CNN's *Paula Zahn,* NBC's *The Today Show, The Early Show* on CBS, National Public Radio, BBC London, ABC Australia, and *Canada A.M.* A frequently requested keynote speaker, he's been invited to address large audiences at book fairs, churches, temples, adult education programs, and nonprofit groups in more than twenty states. He has also written original articles in over thirty-five magazines, fifty newspapers, and more than fifty online websites and newsletters.

Originally from Detroit, Michigan, Dr. Felder graduated with high honors from Kenyon College in Ohio. Prior to becoming a psychologist, he was the director of research for Doubleday and Company in New York and the manager of strategic planning for American Express at their corporate headquarters. He has also been a consultant for numerous nonprofit and educational organizations.

Dr. Felder received the 1985 Nonfiction Book of the Year Award from *Medical Self-Care Magazine,* the 2002 Best Spiritual Writing Award from *Tikkun Magazine,* and a 2005 honorary degree from the New Seminary in New York for developing methods to teach clergy and congregations to be respectful of diversity. Active in several volunteer organizations, he has received the Distinguished Merit Citation of the National Conference of Christians and Jews for developing programs to overcome racism, sexism, homophobia, and religious prejudice.

Dr. Felder and his wife, visual artist Linda Schorin, have been together for twenty-eight years and are the parents of a child who has special needs. They live in Mar Vista, California.